ETHEREAL BIRDS AND BUTTERFLIES

A Unique Coloring Book for Adults

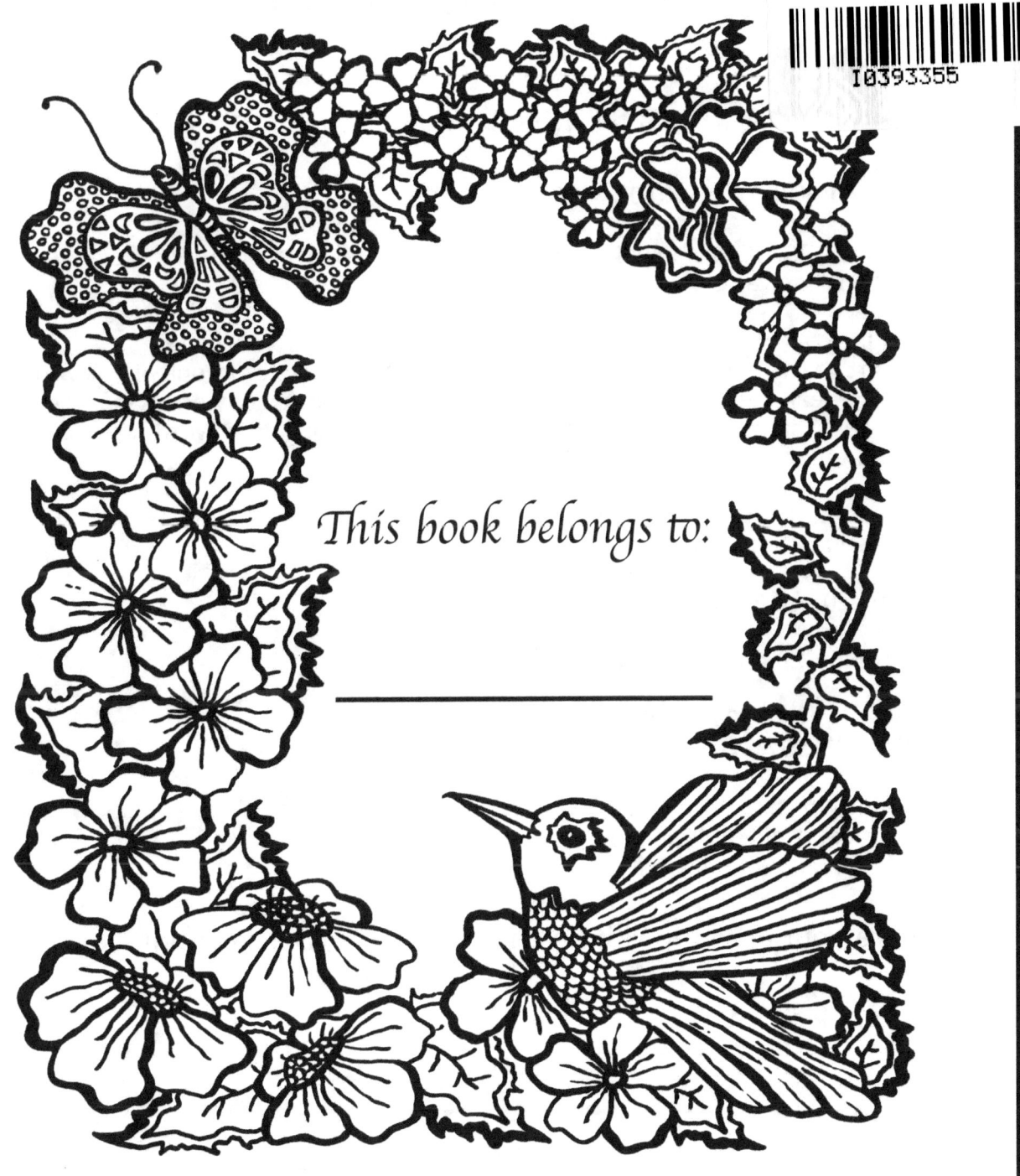

This book belongs to:

_____

More Than 40 Hand-Drawn Designs by Olivia Schiopu

Ethereal Birds and Butterflies: A Unique Coloring Book for Adults

Original Illustrations by Olivia Schiopu
Book and Cover Design by Ioana Schiopu

Manufactured in Canada

Printed by CreateSpace, An Amazon.com Company

ISBN-13:978-1537173252
ISBN-10:1537173251

coloring@riosart.net
www.riosart.net

Share your artwork with us on Instagram @rioscoloring!

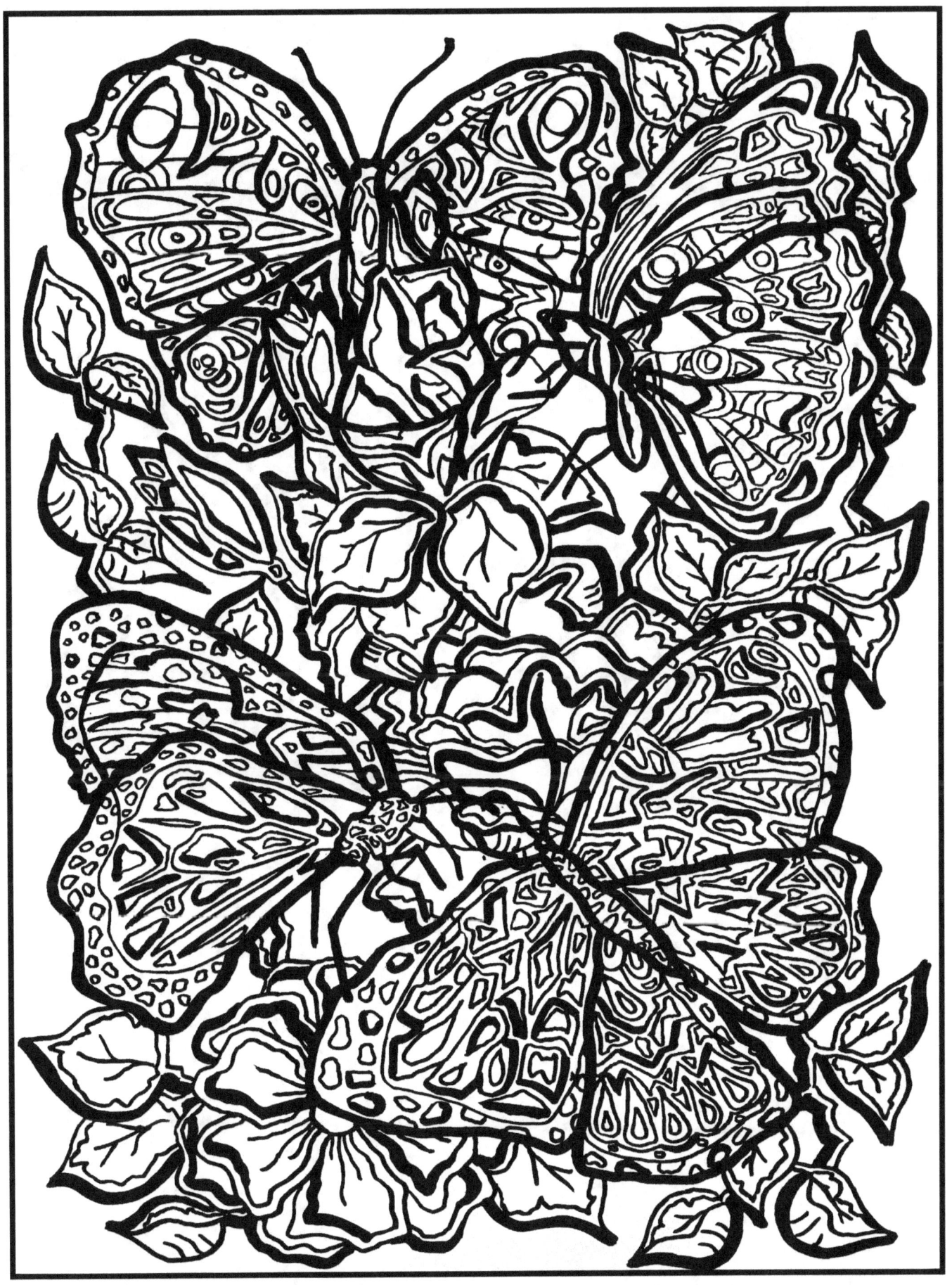

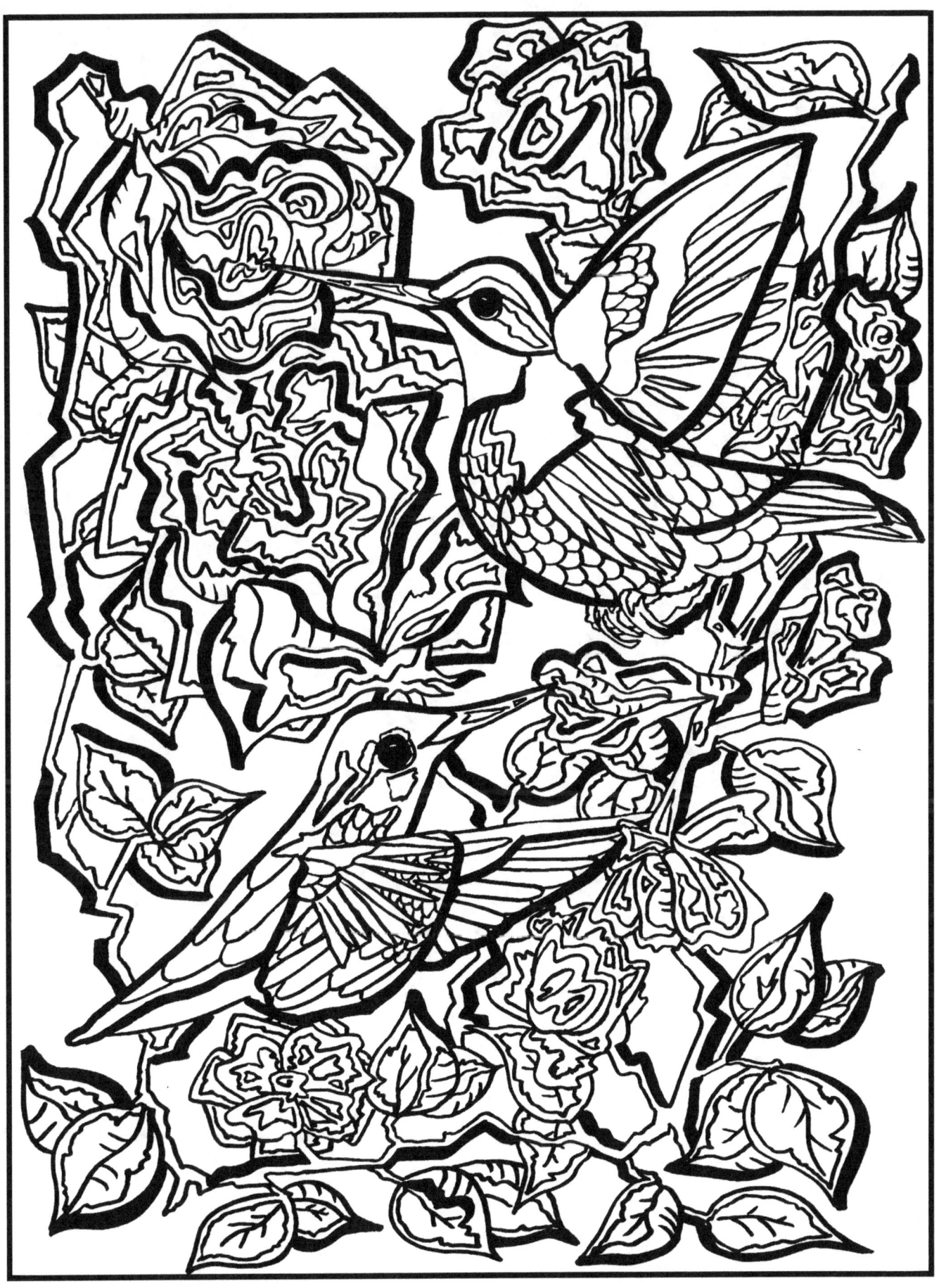

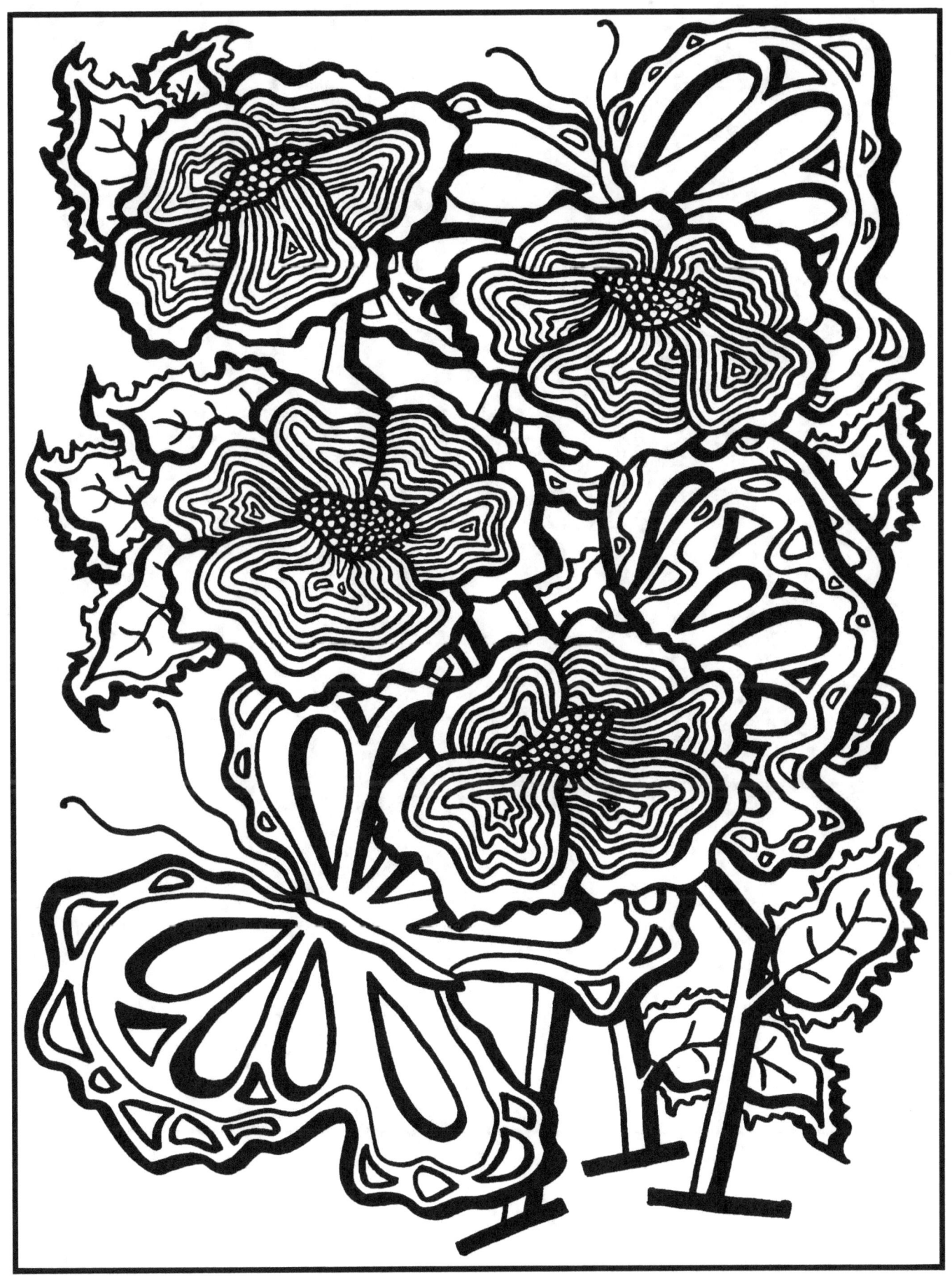

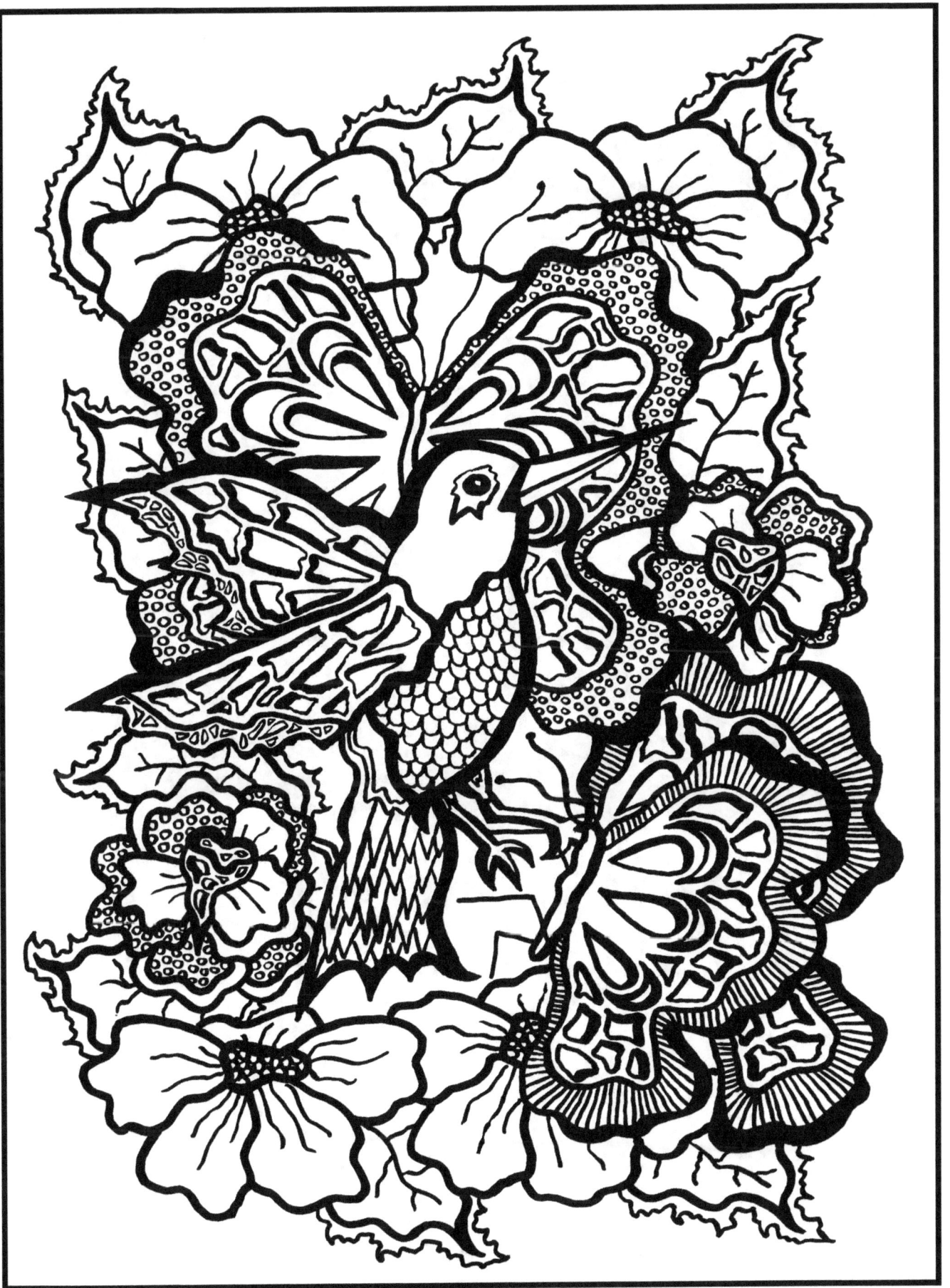

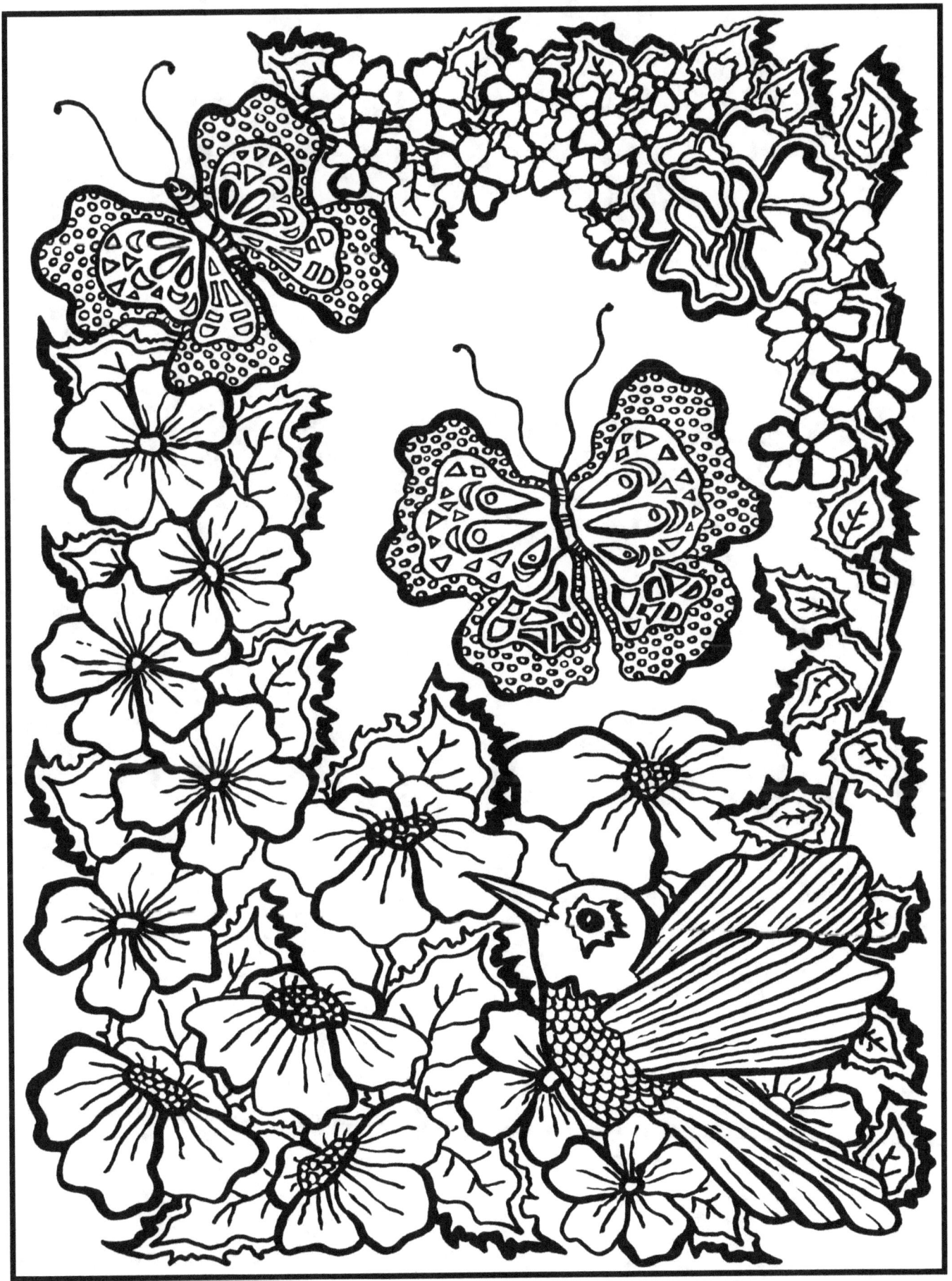

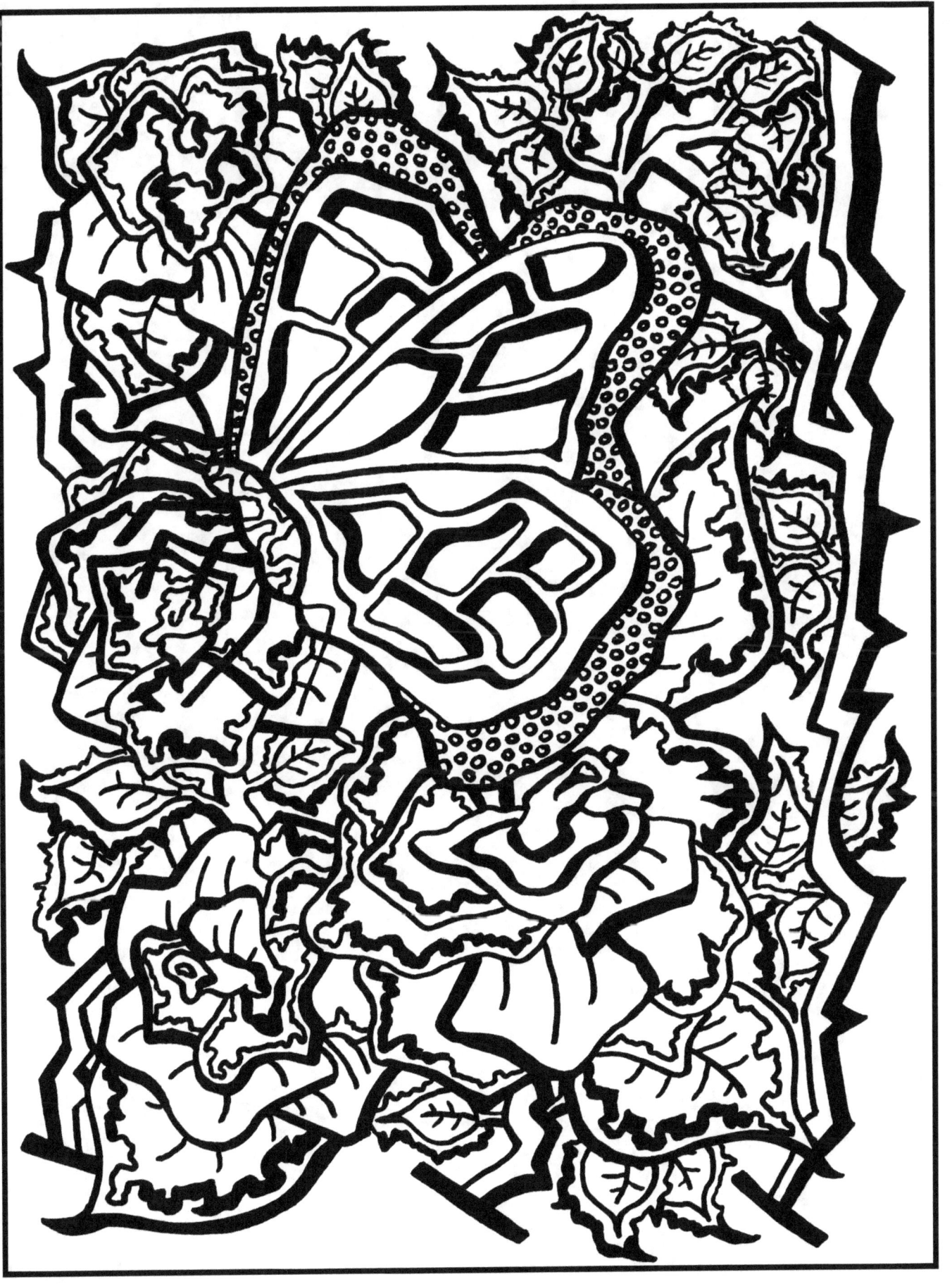

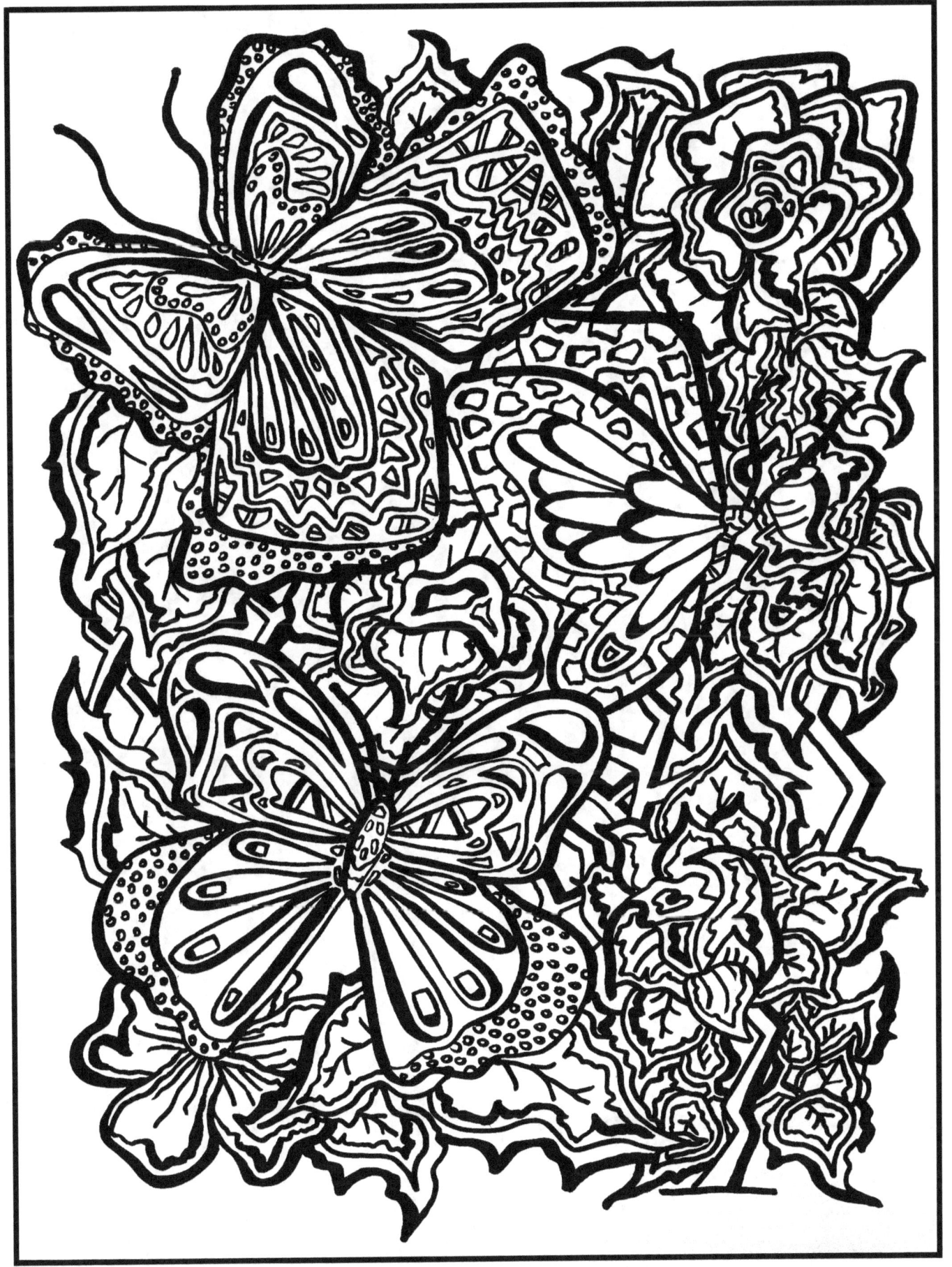

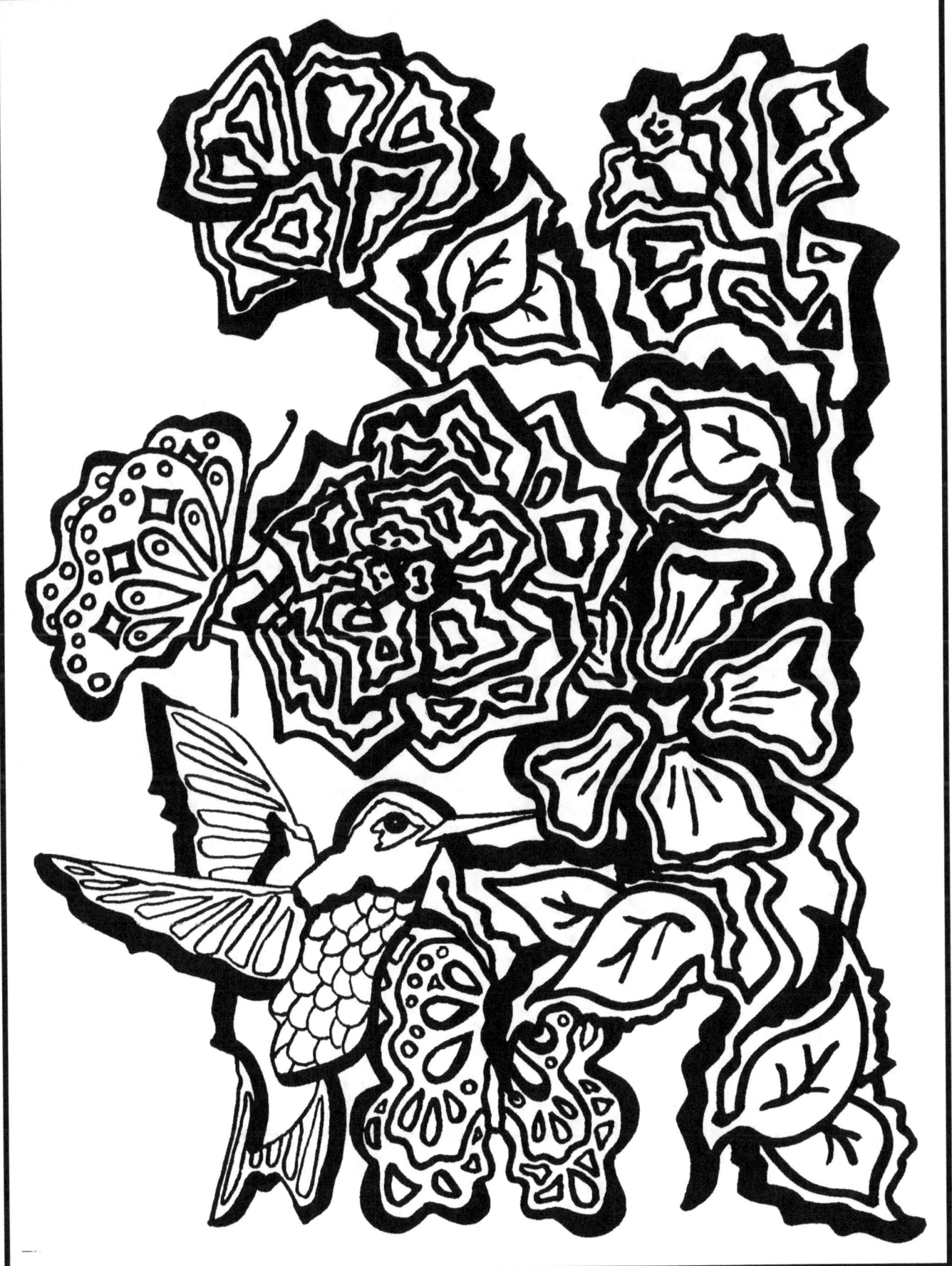

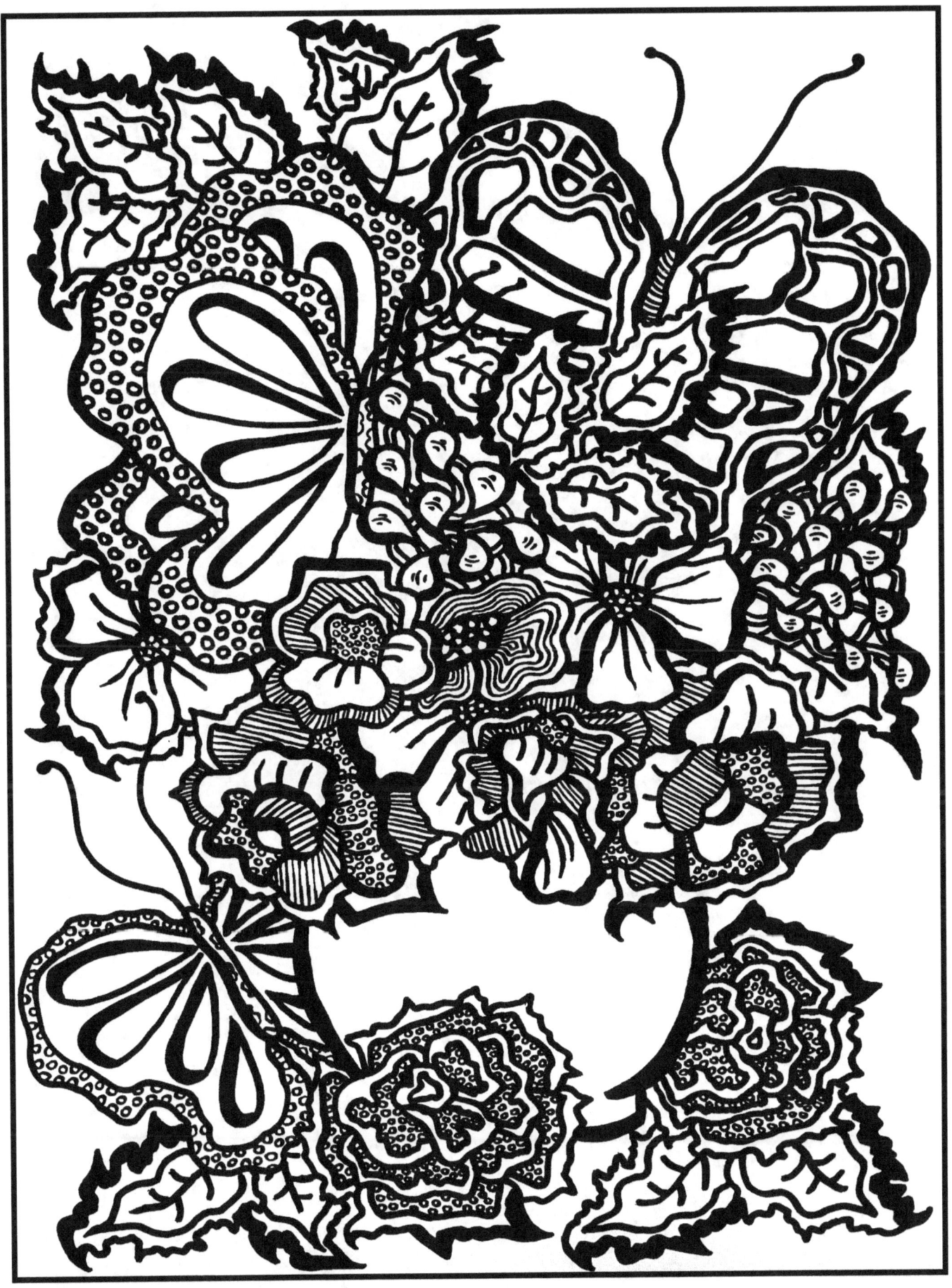

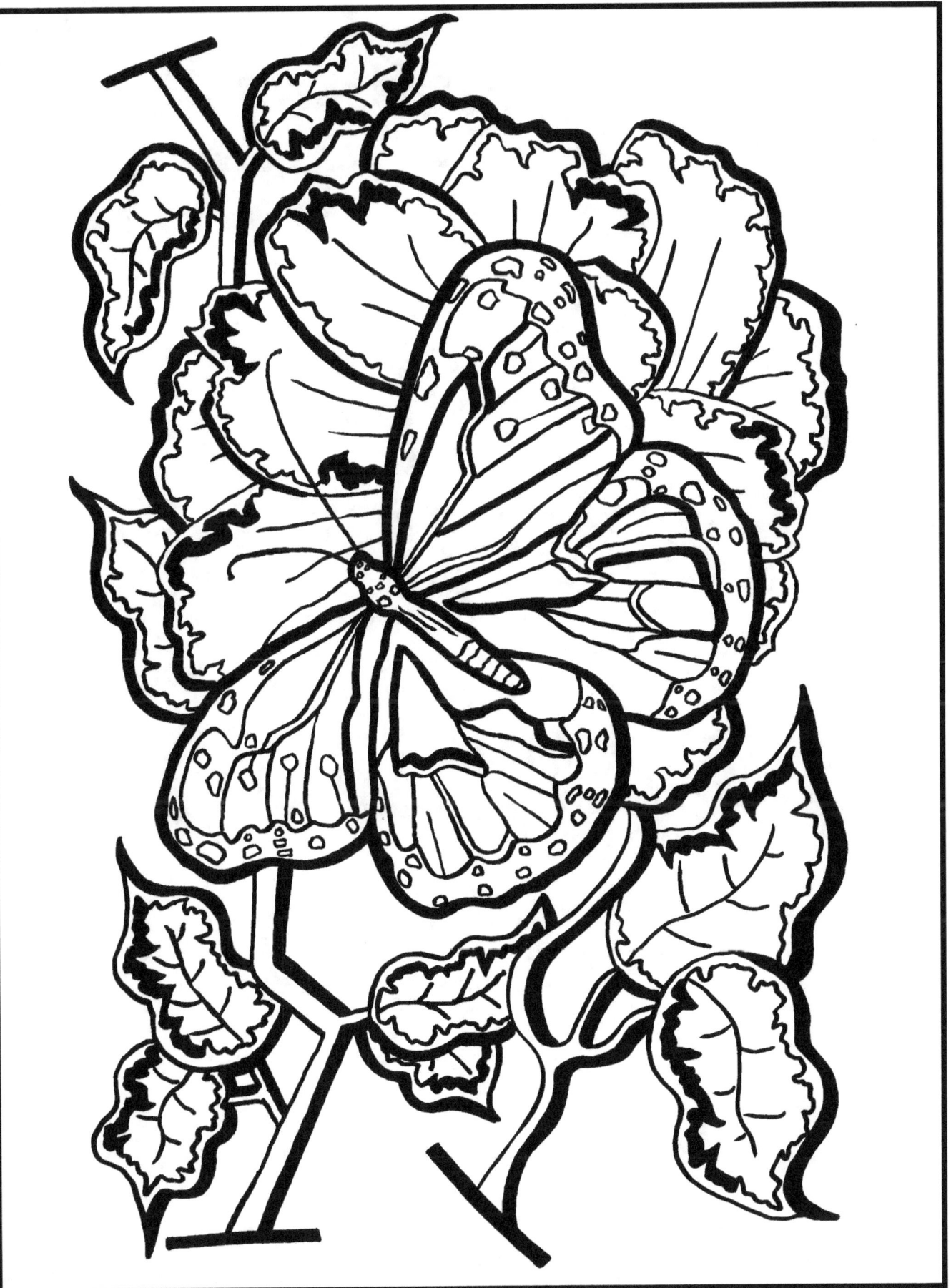

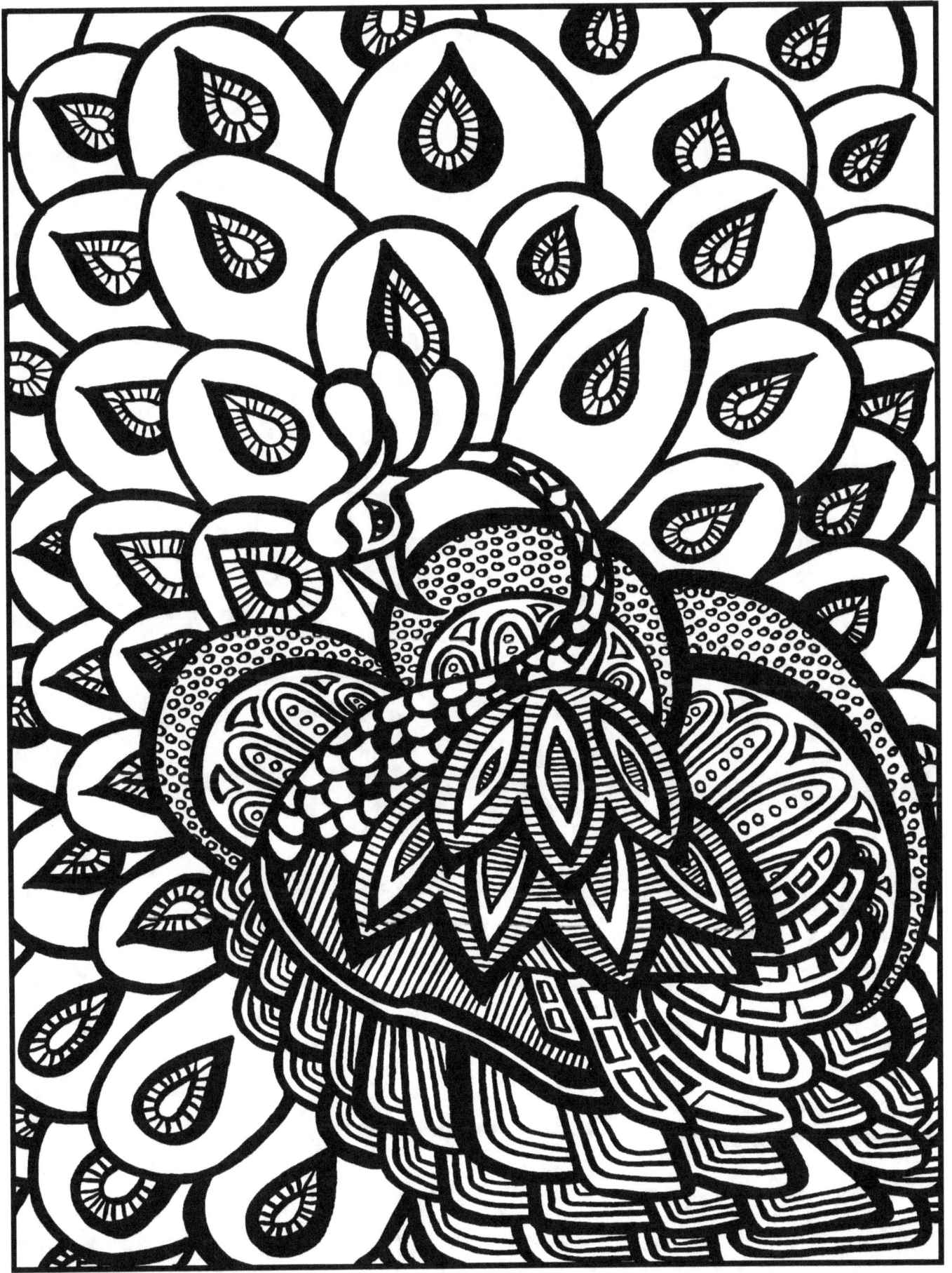

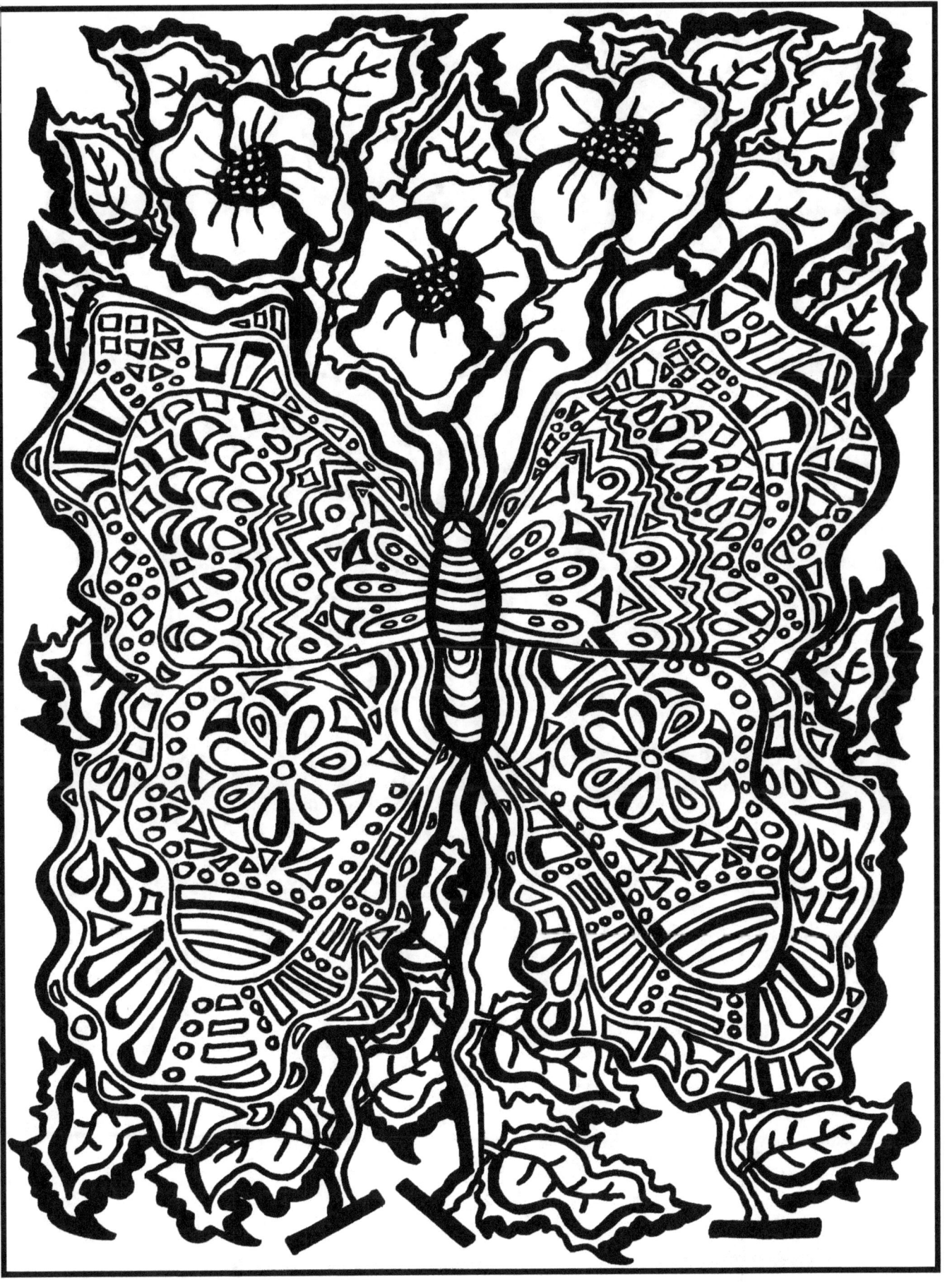

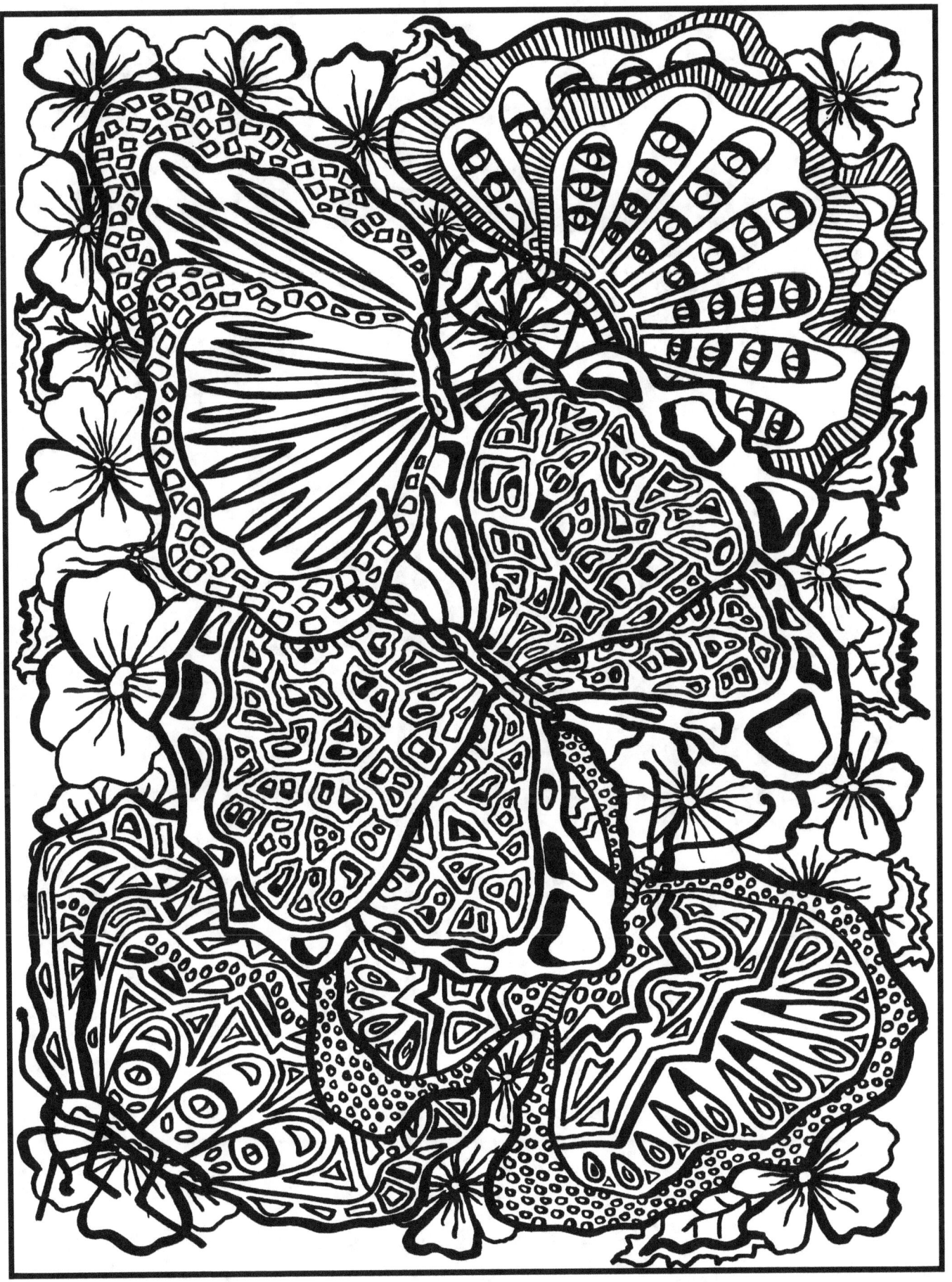

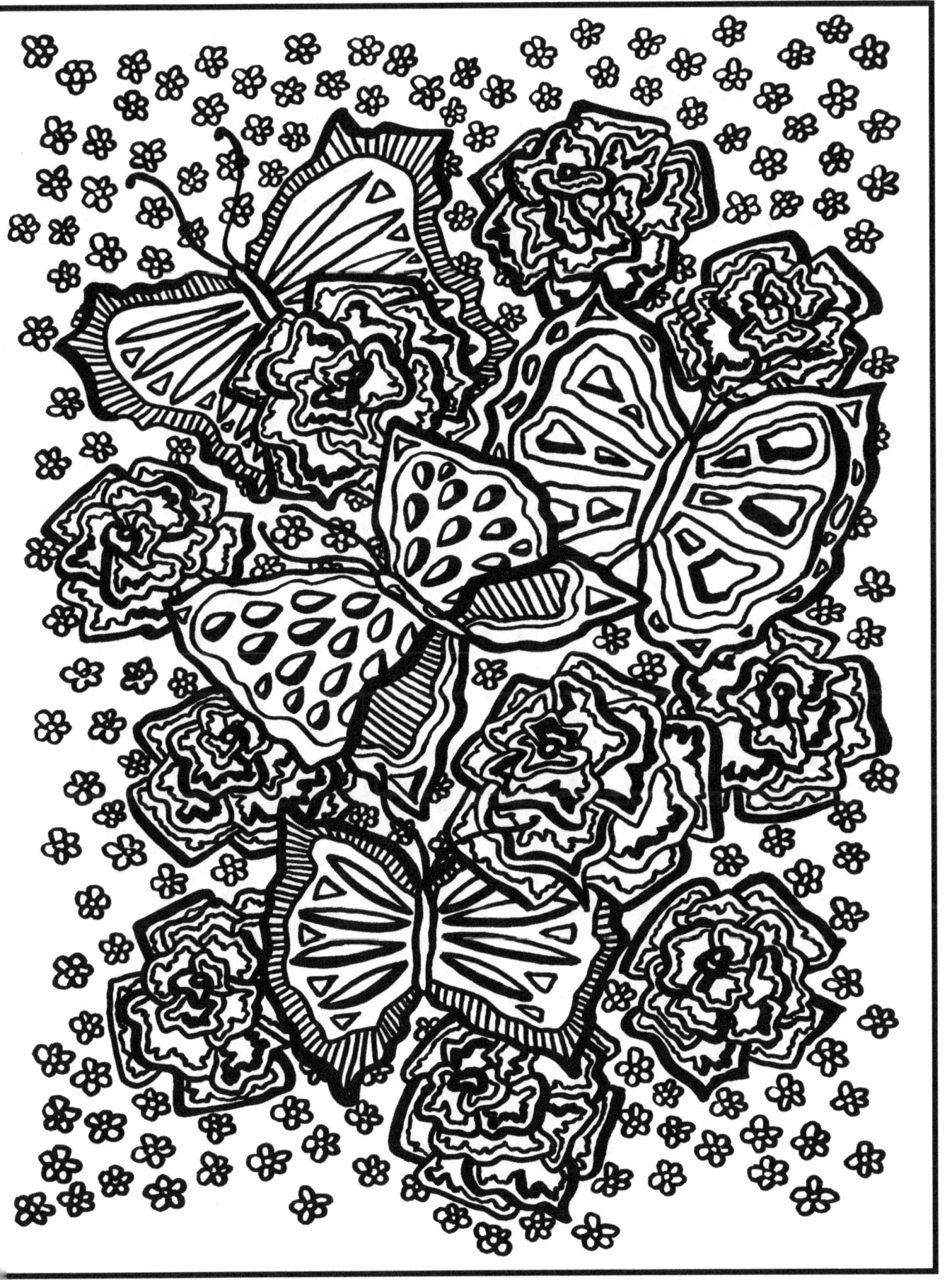

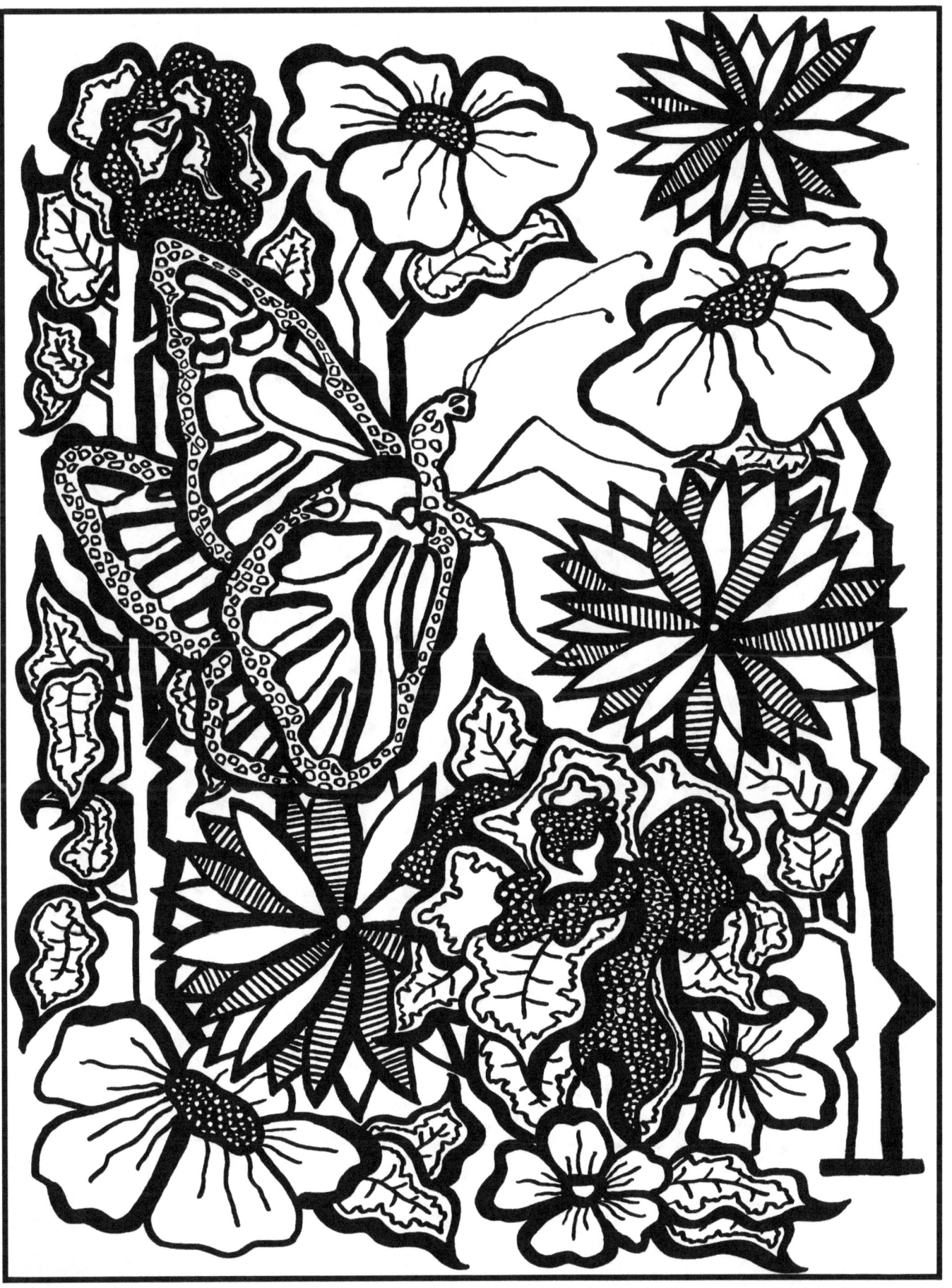

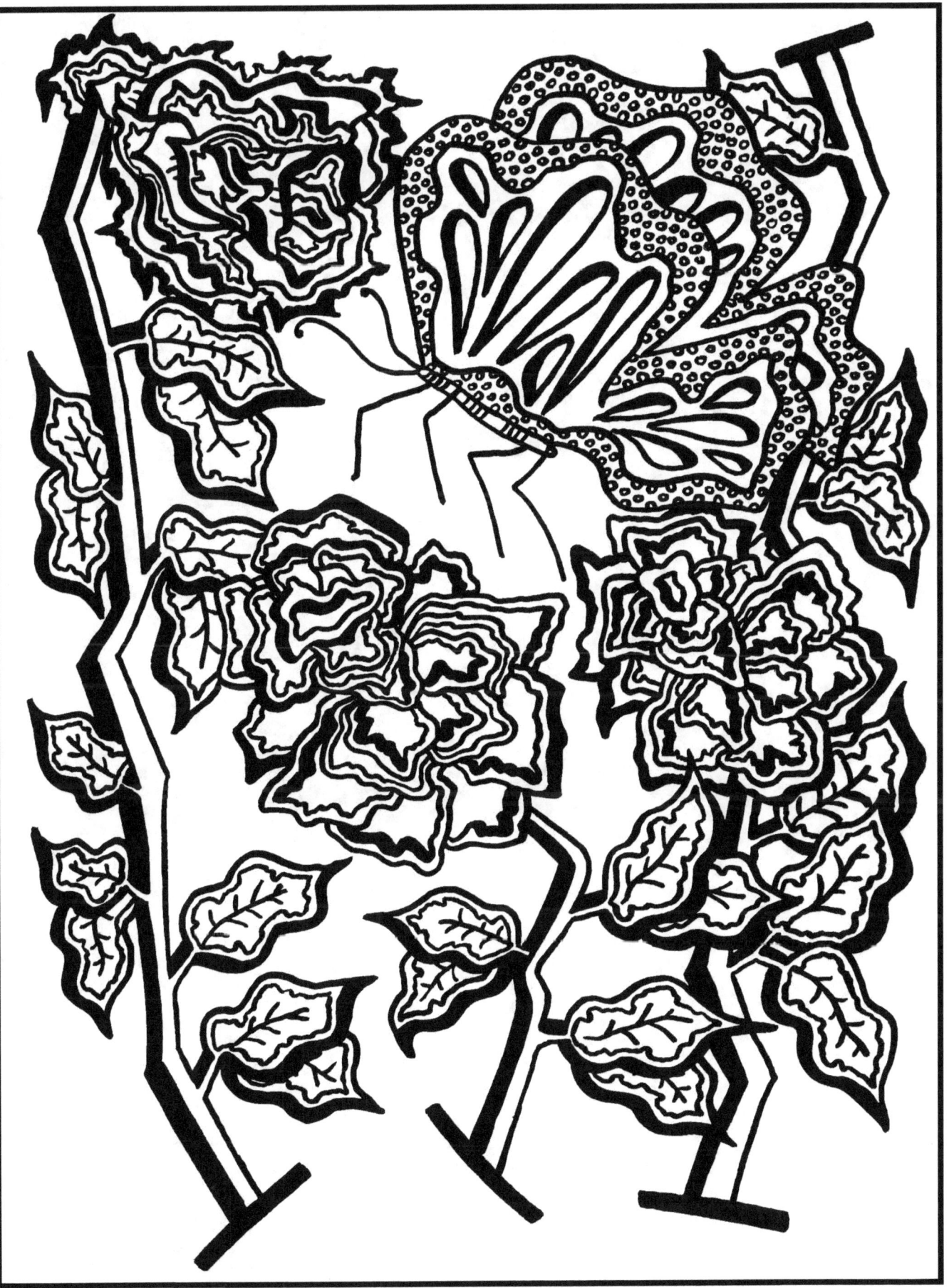

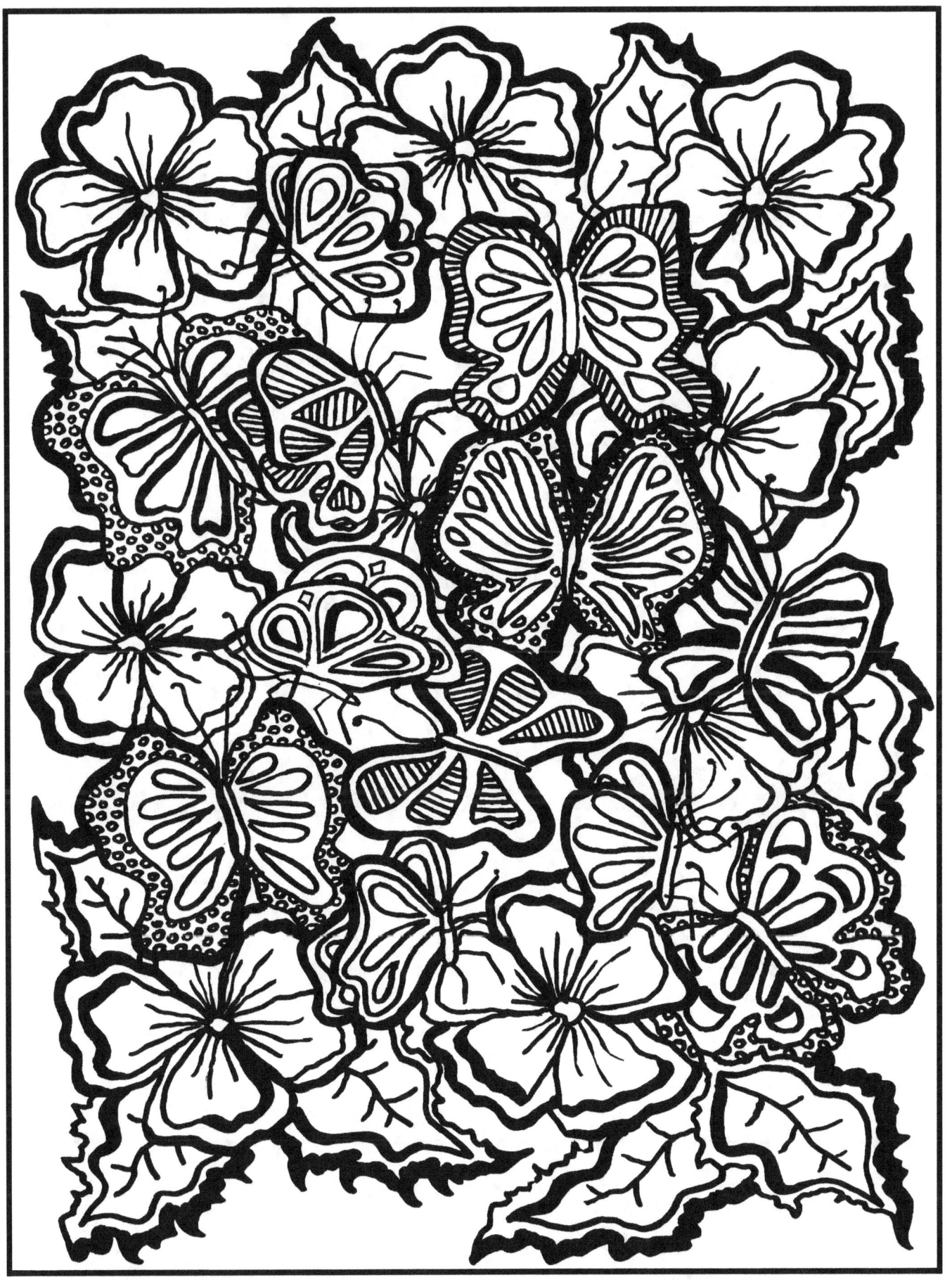

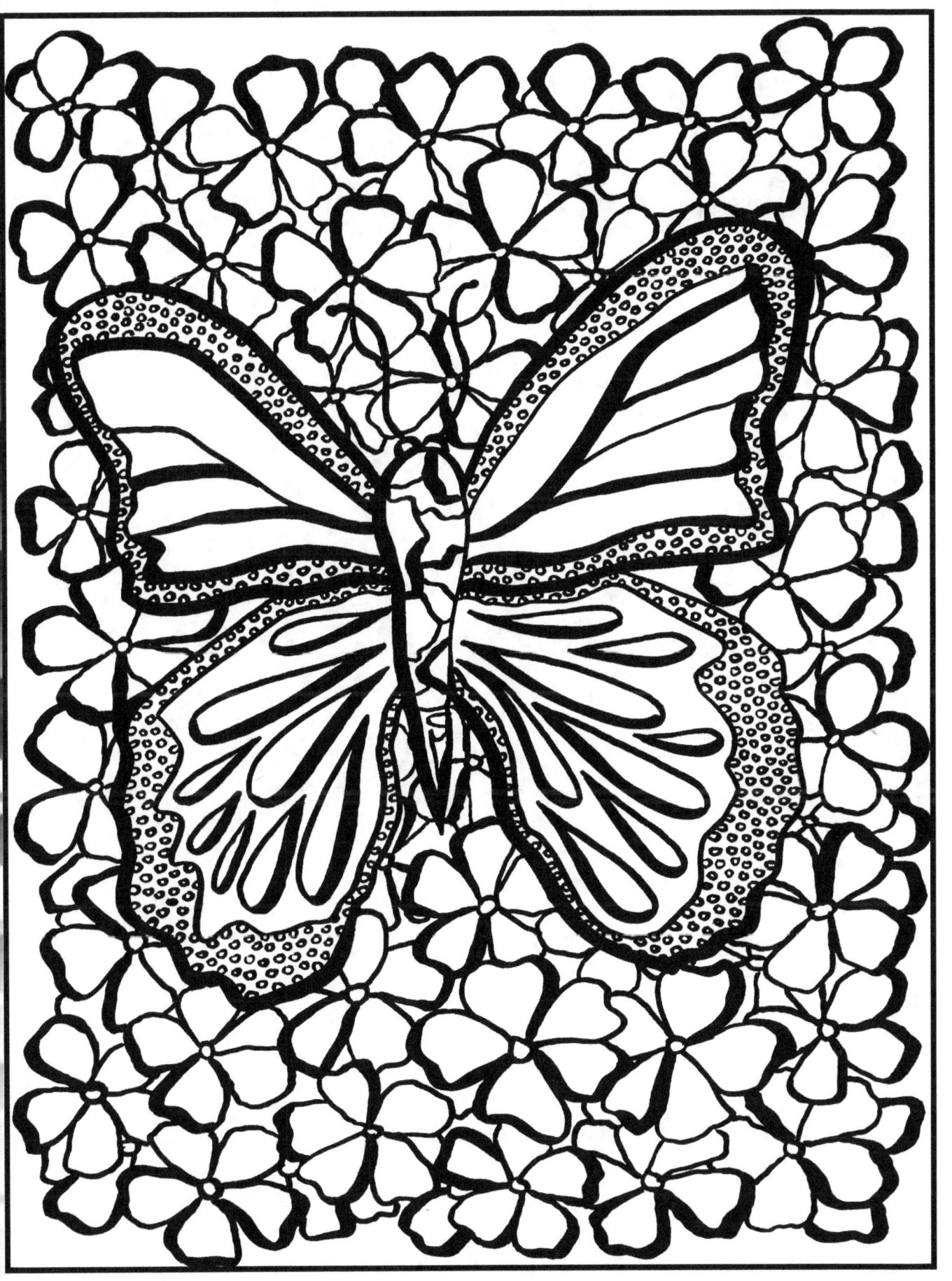

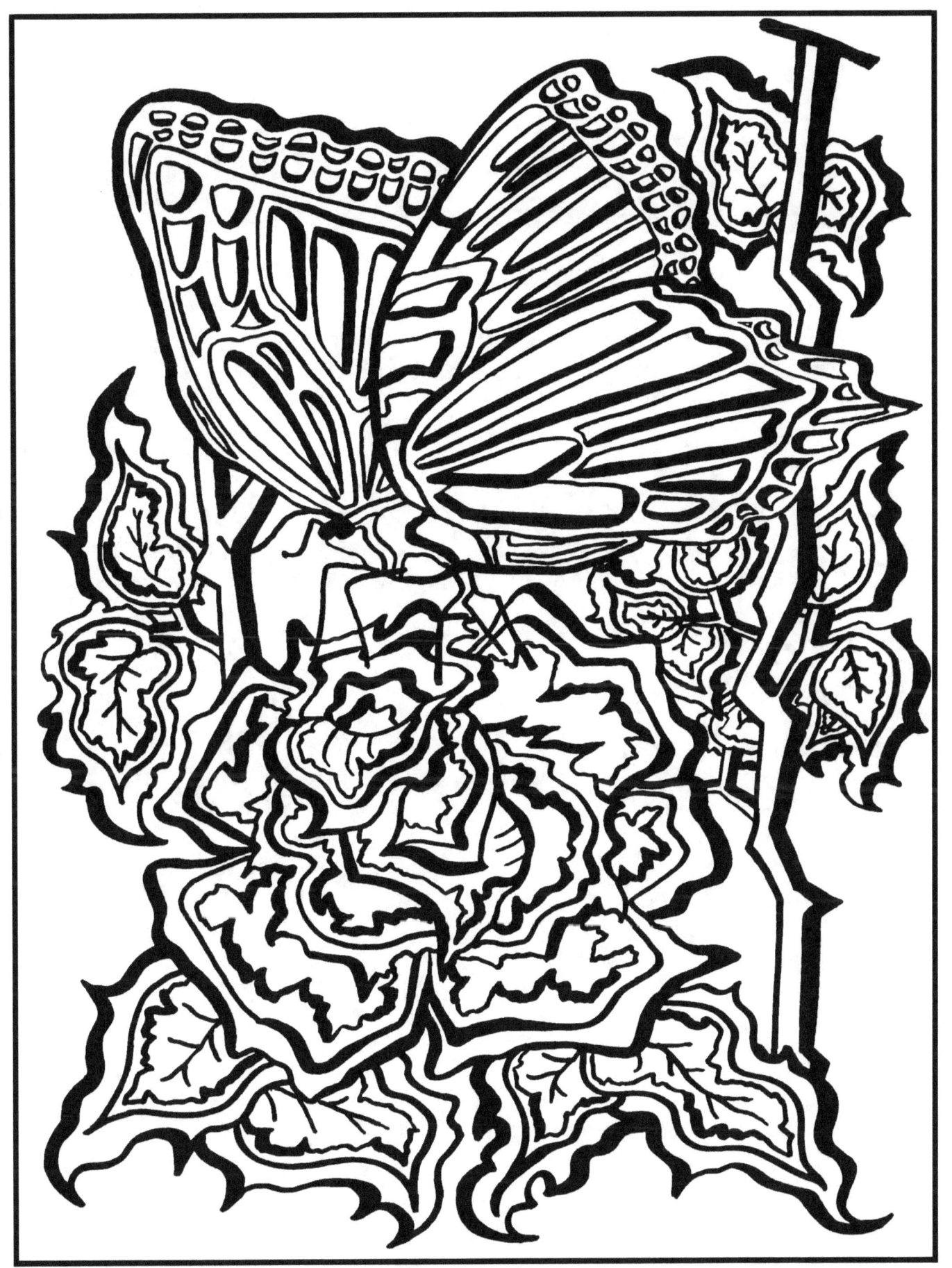

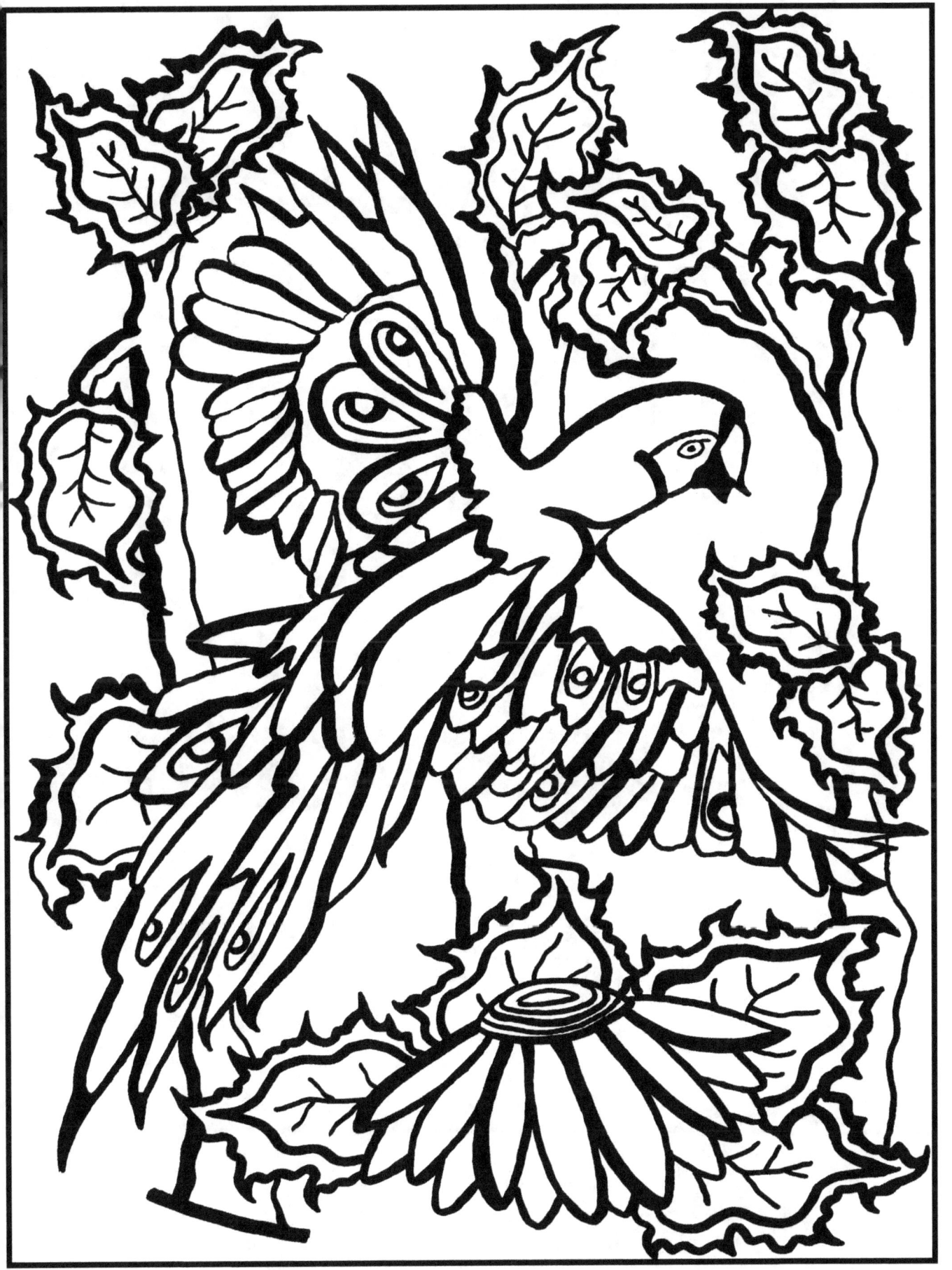

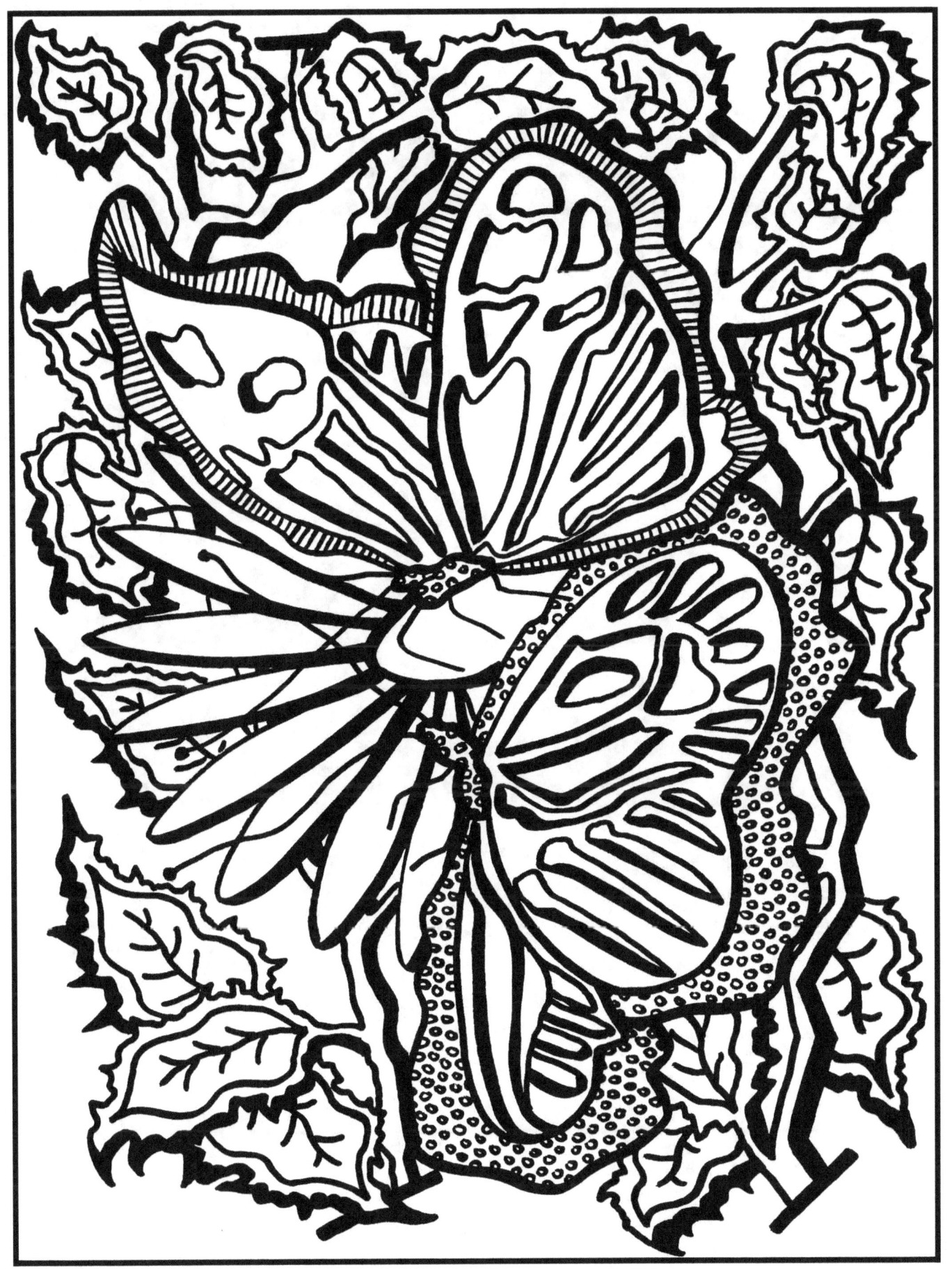

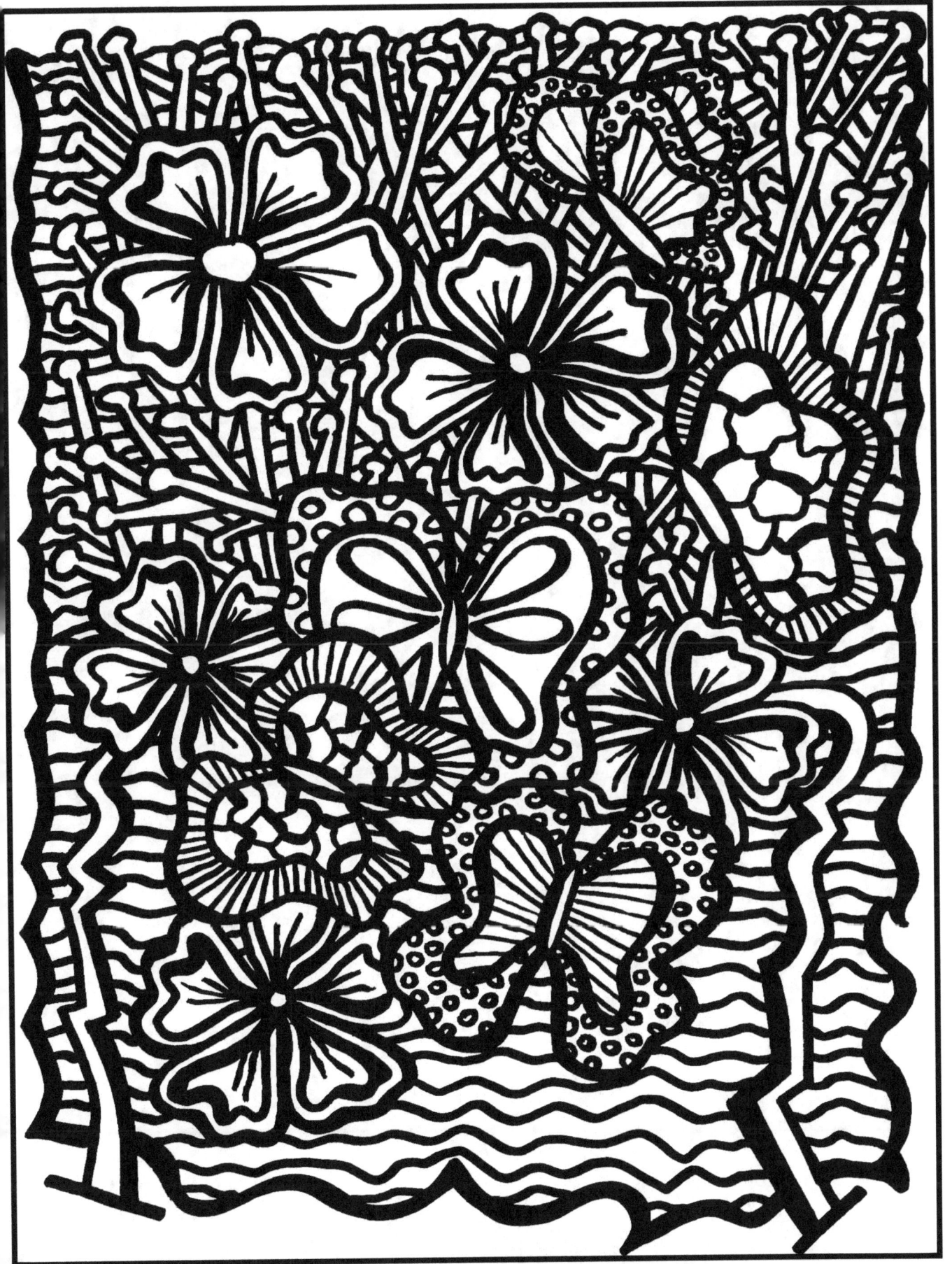

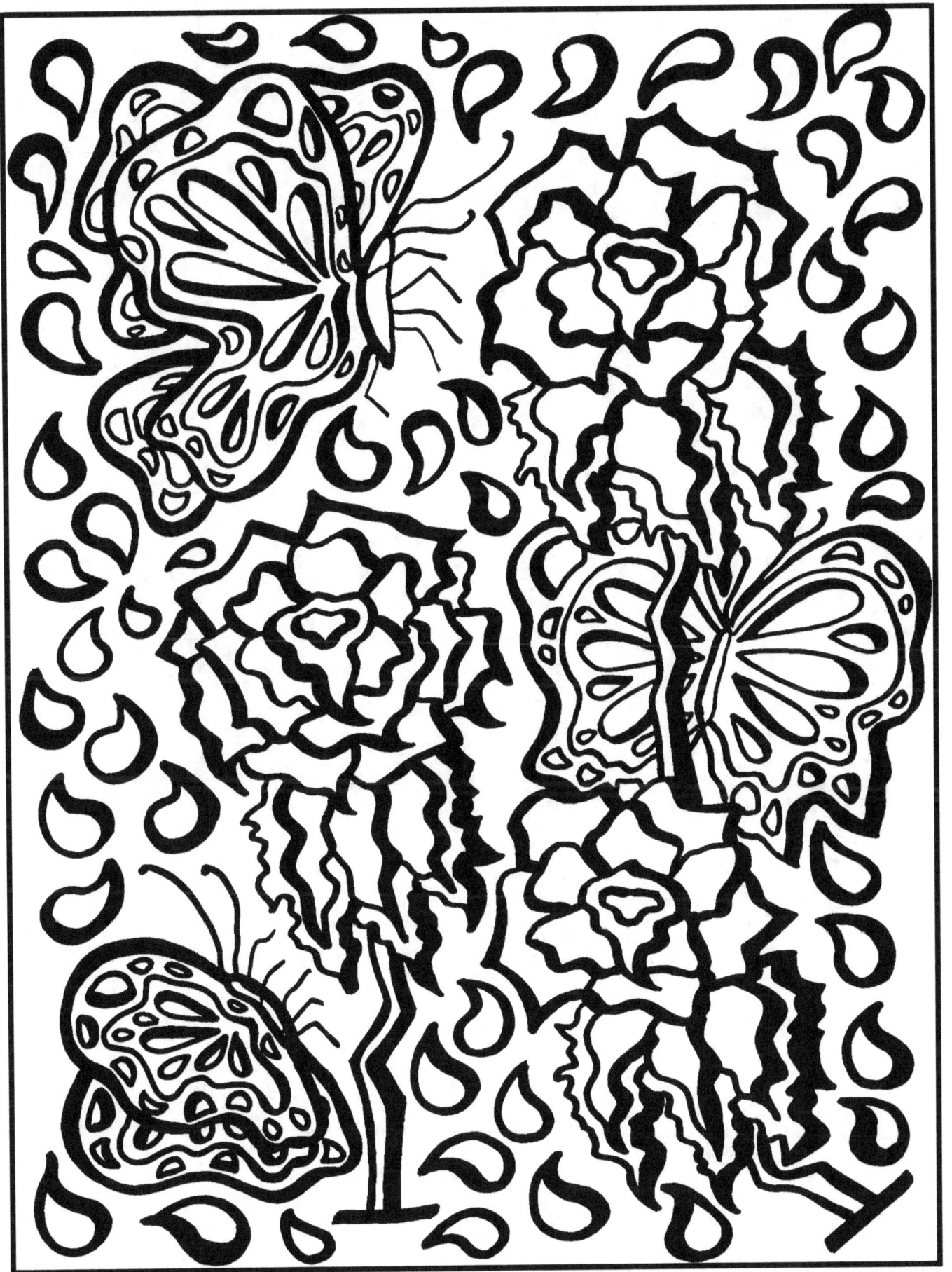

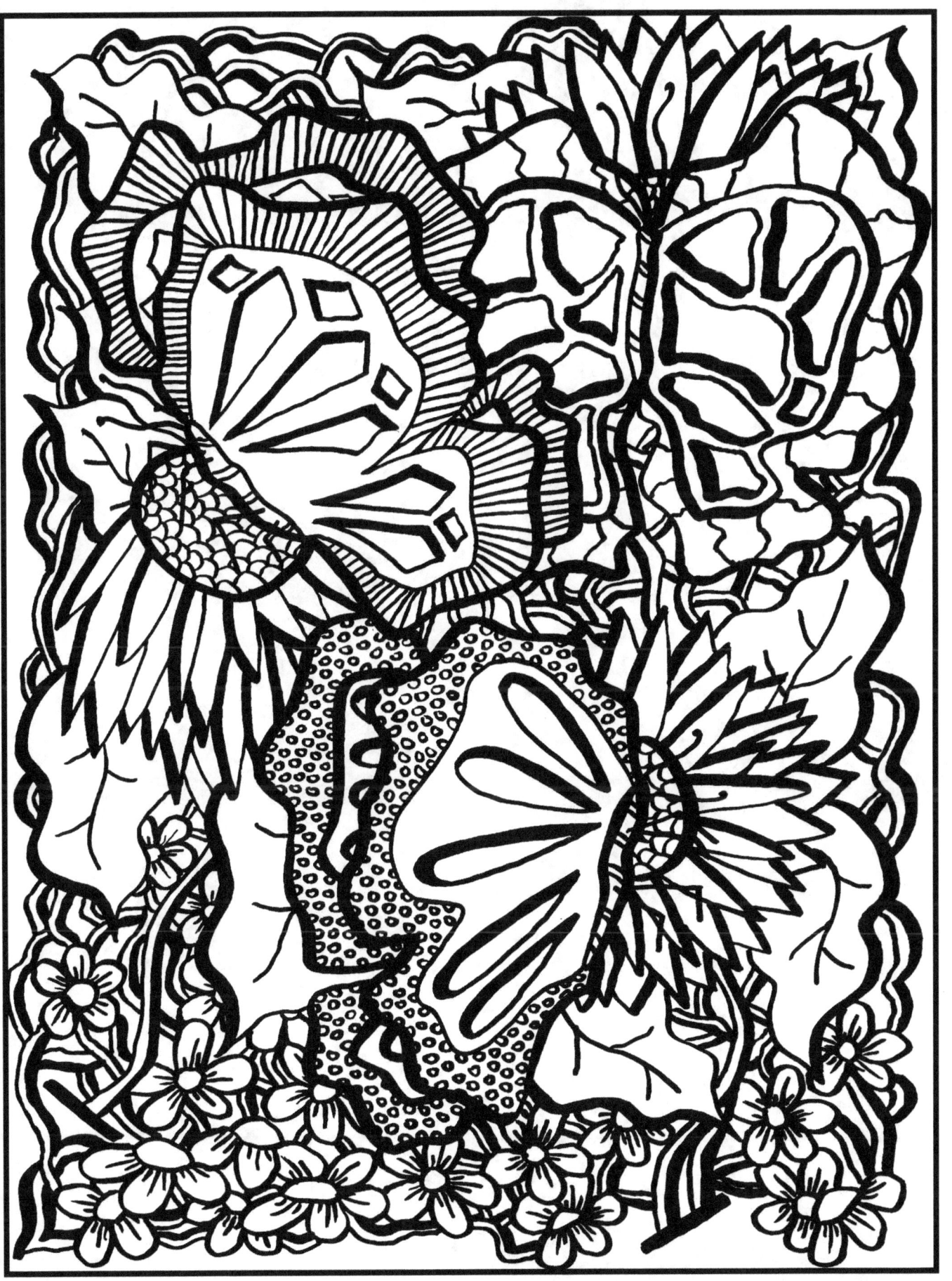

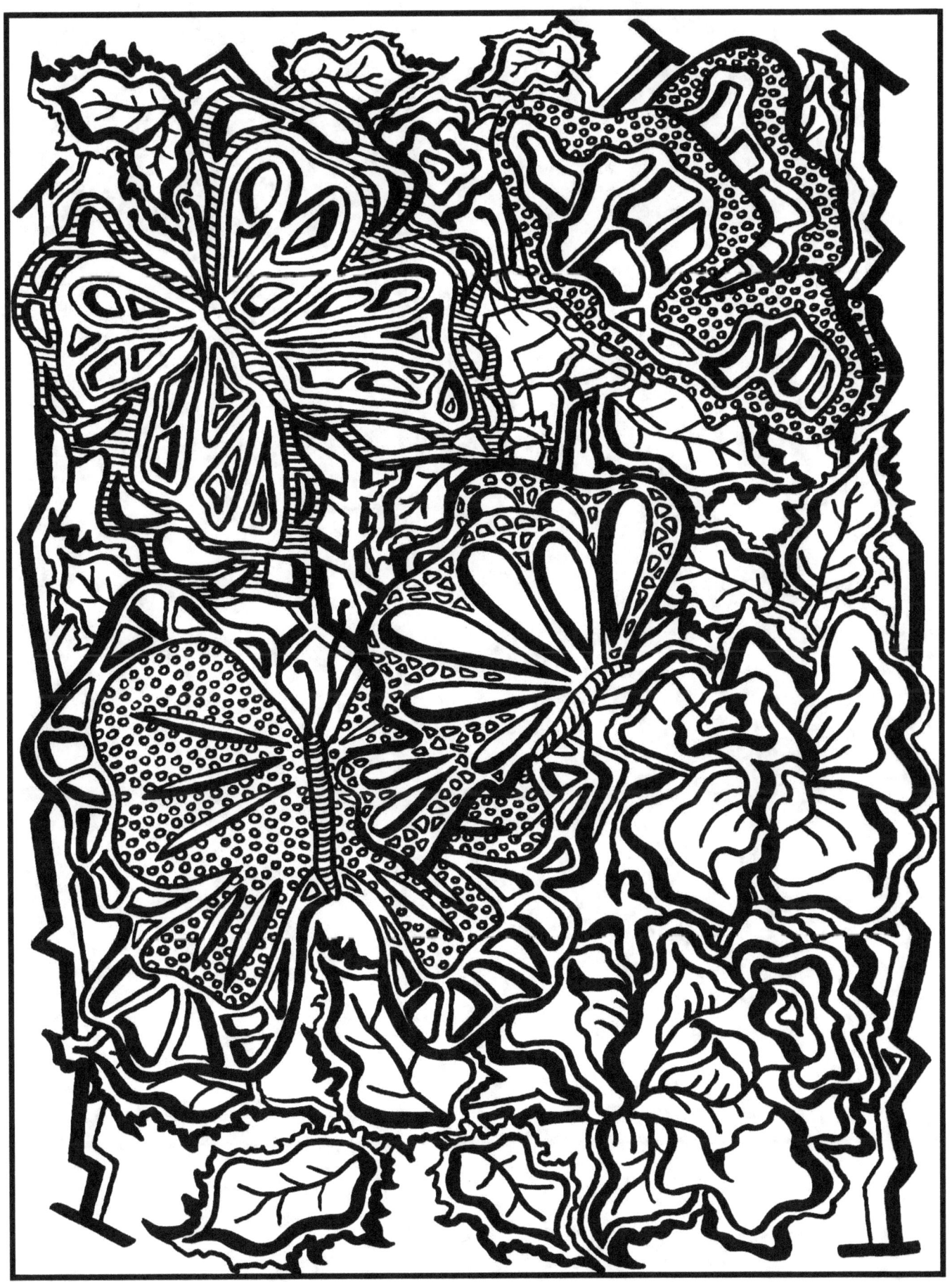

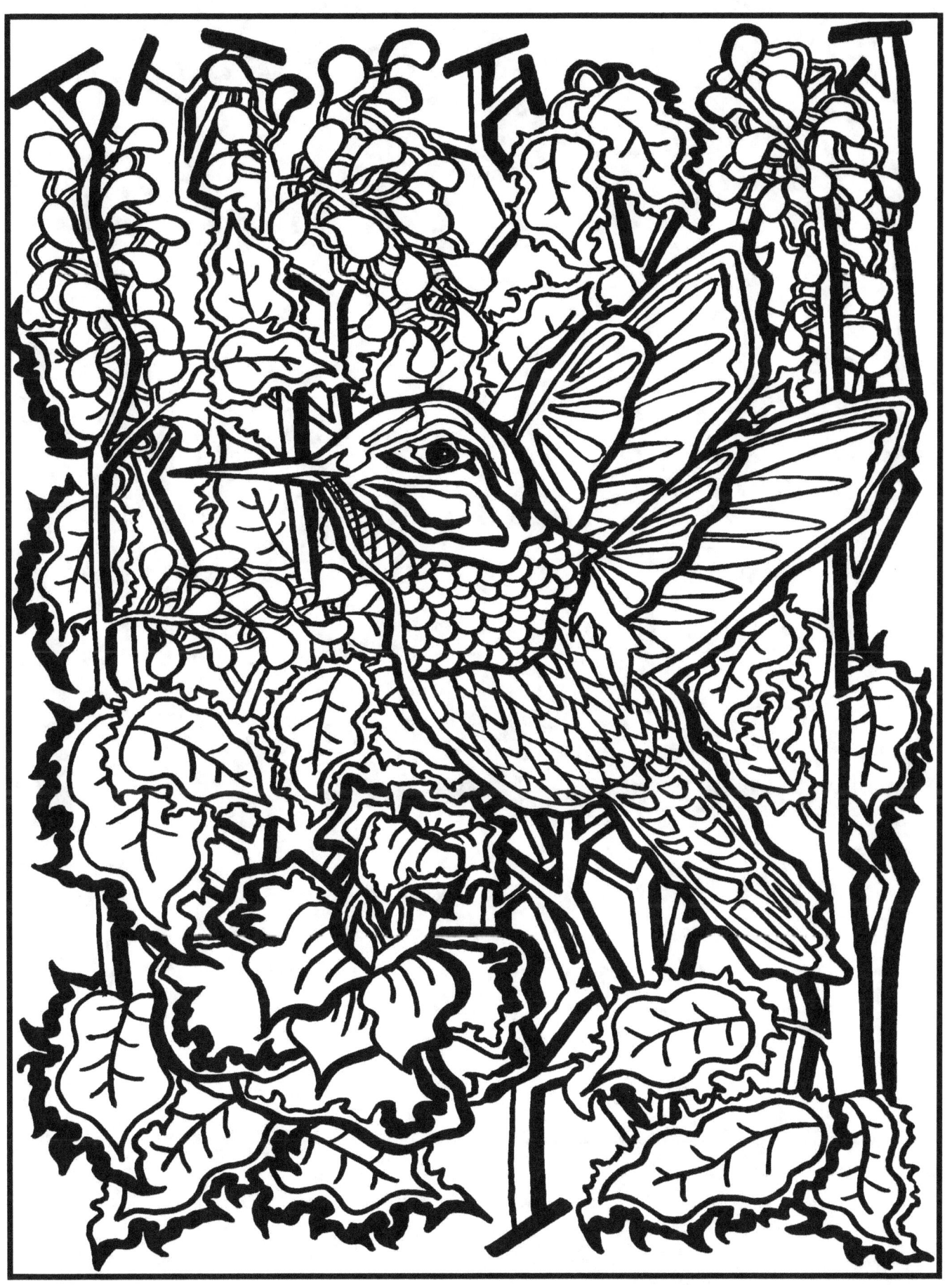

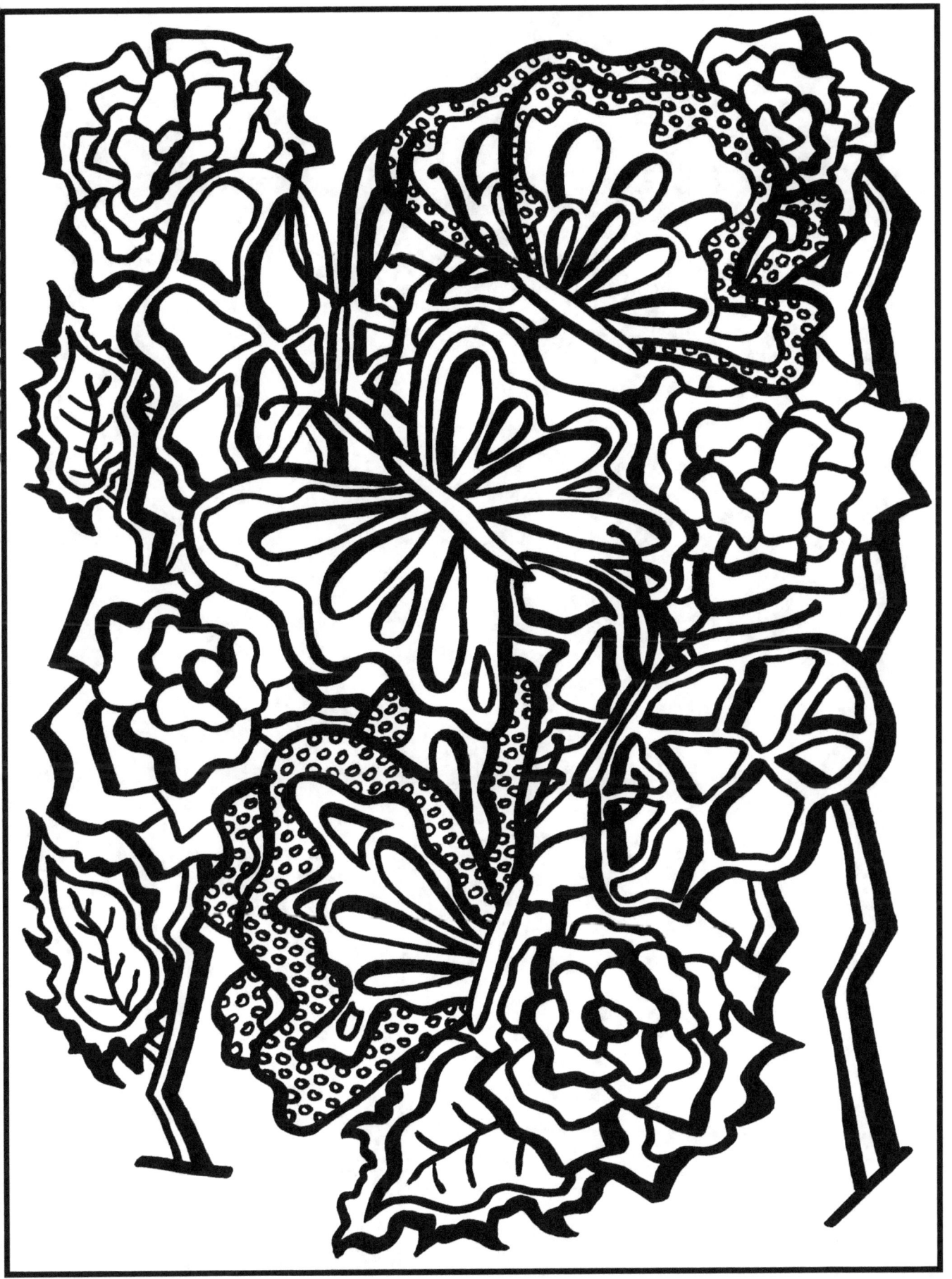

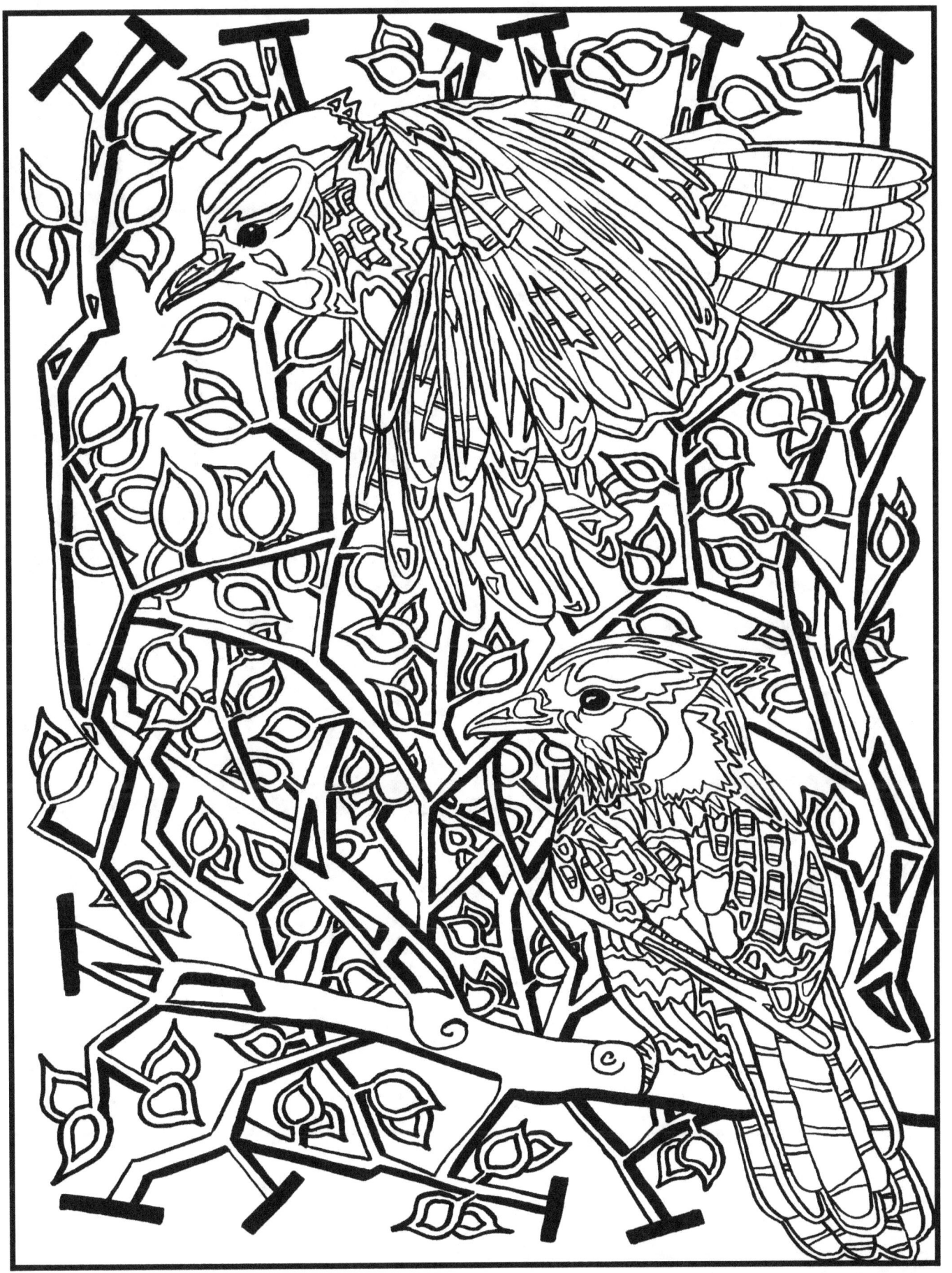

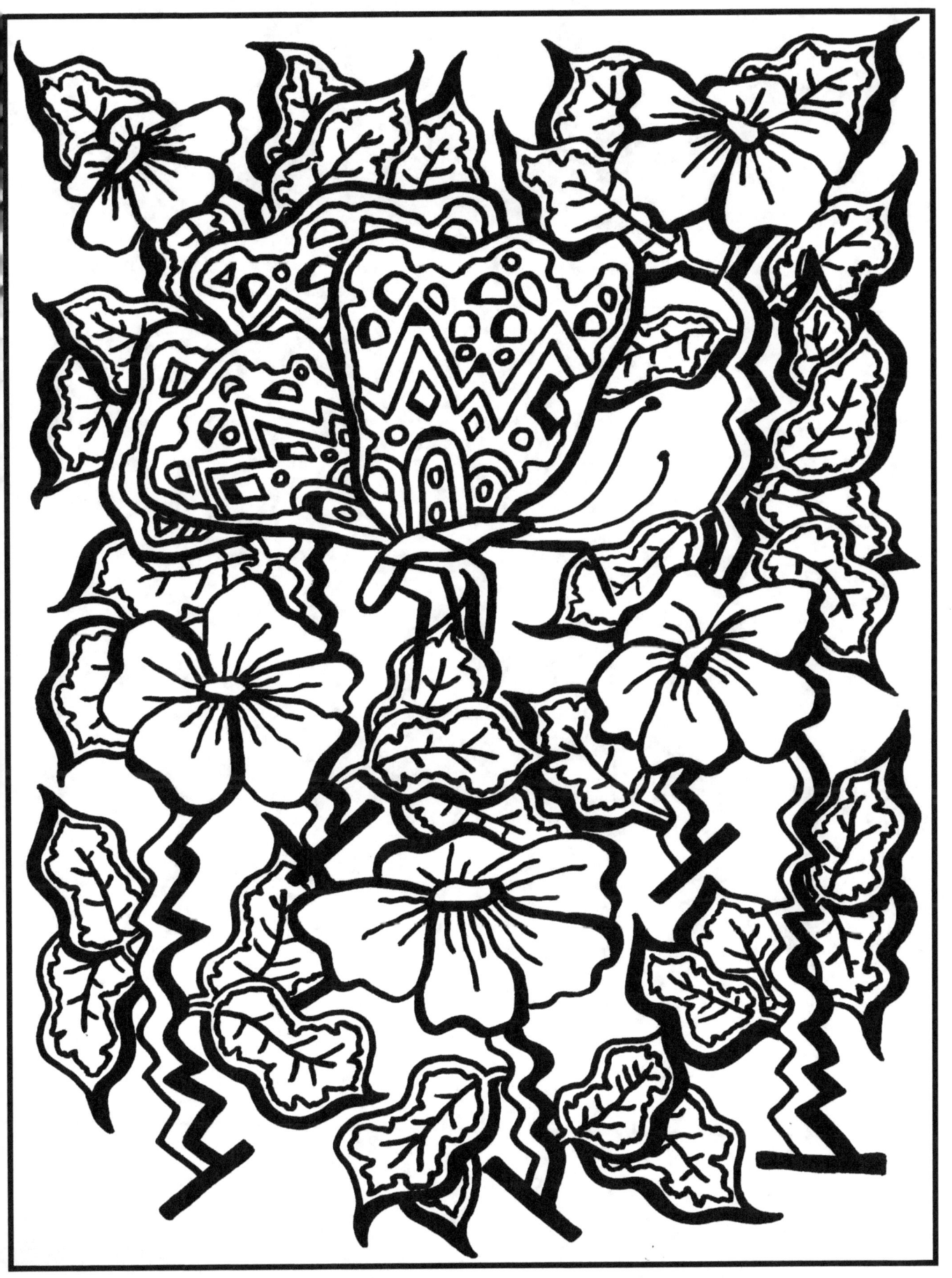

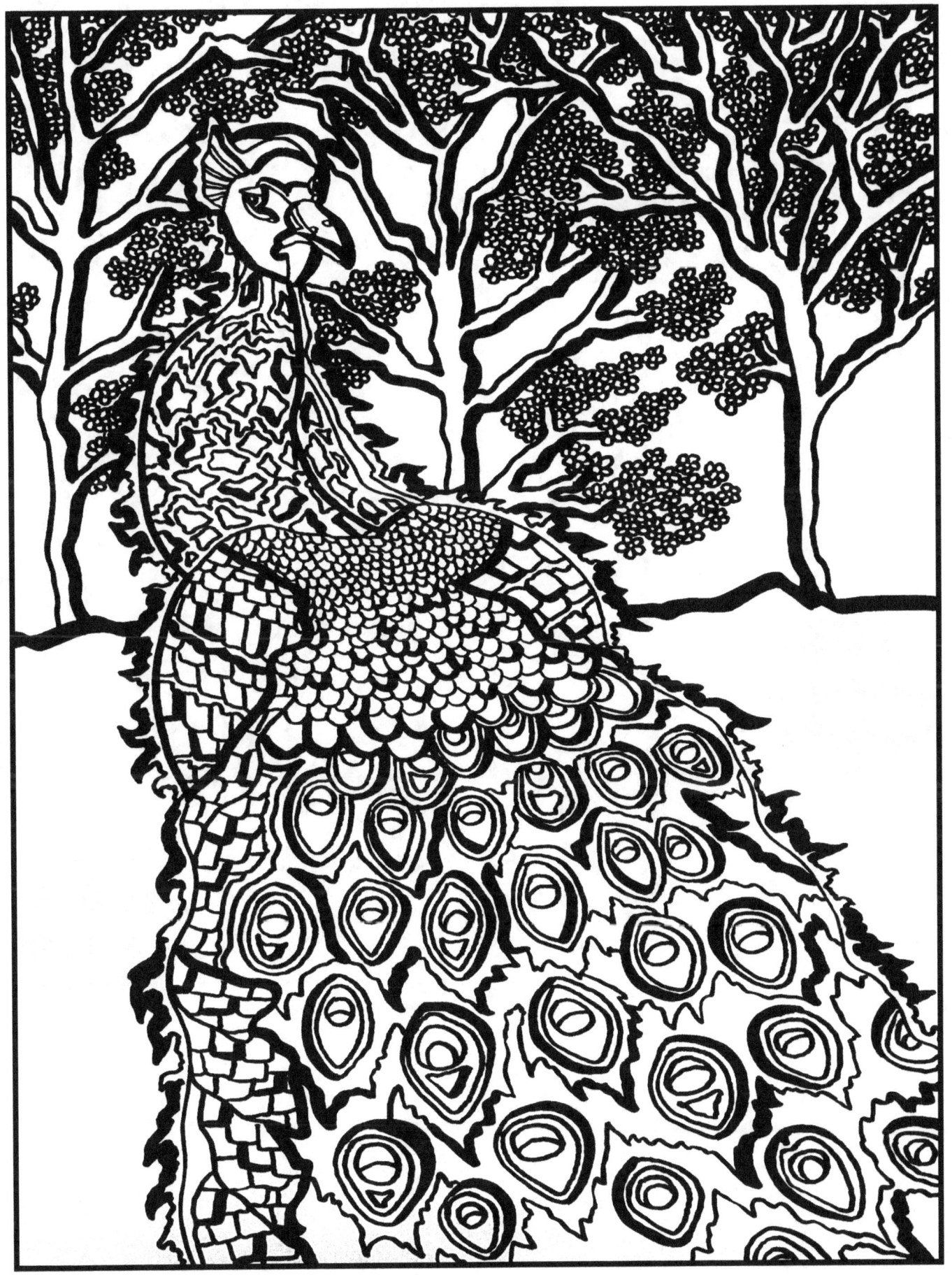

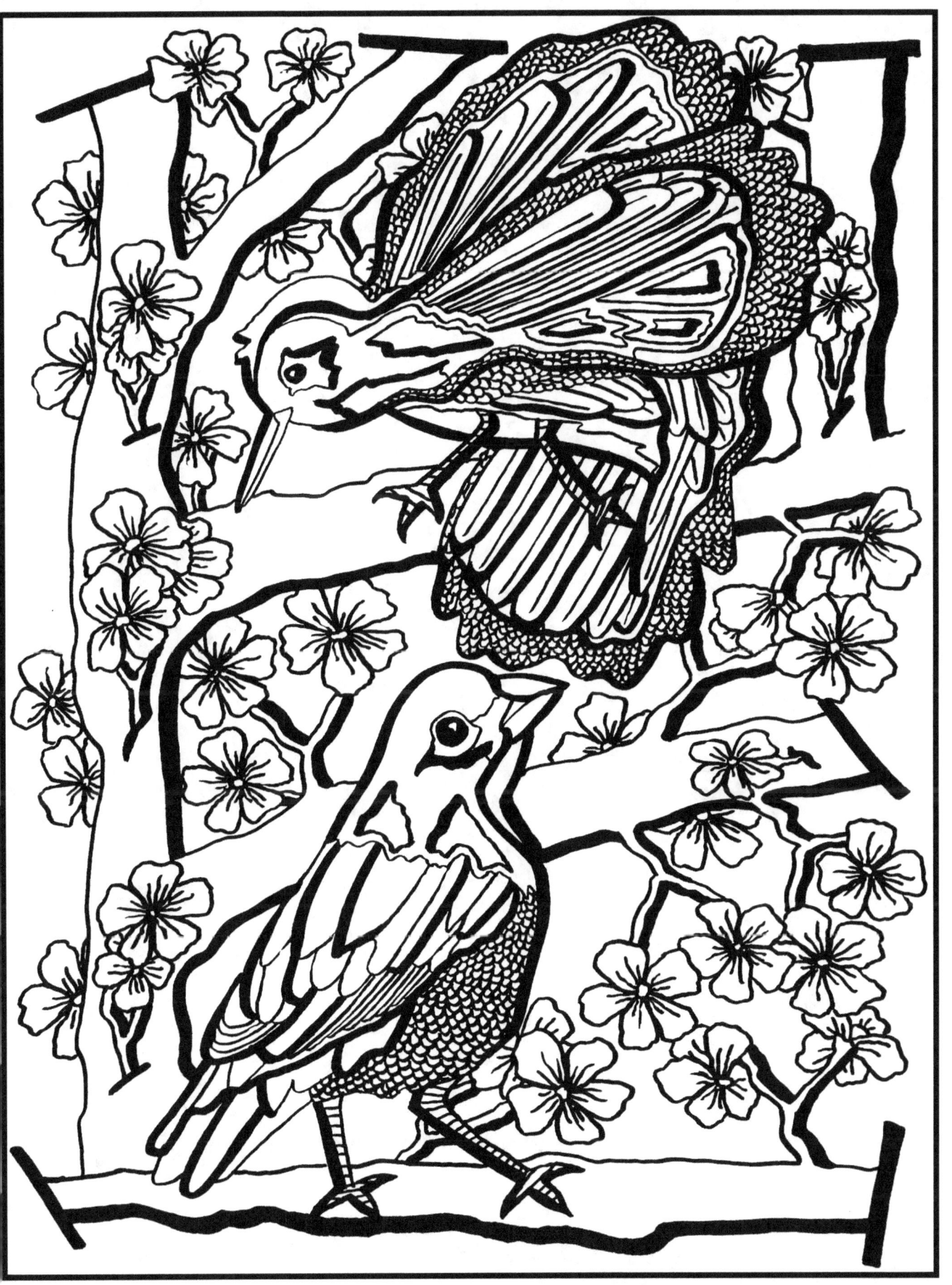

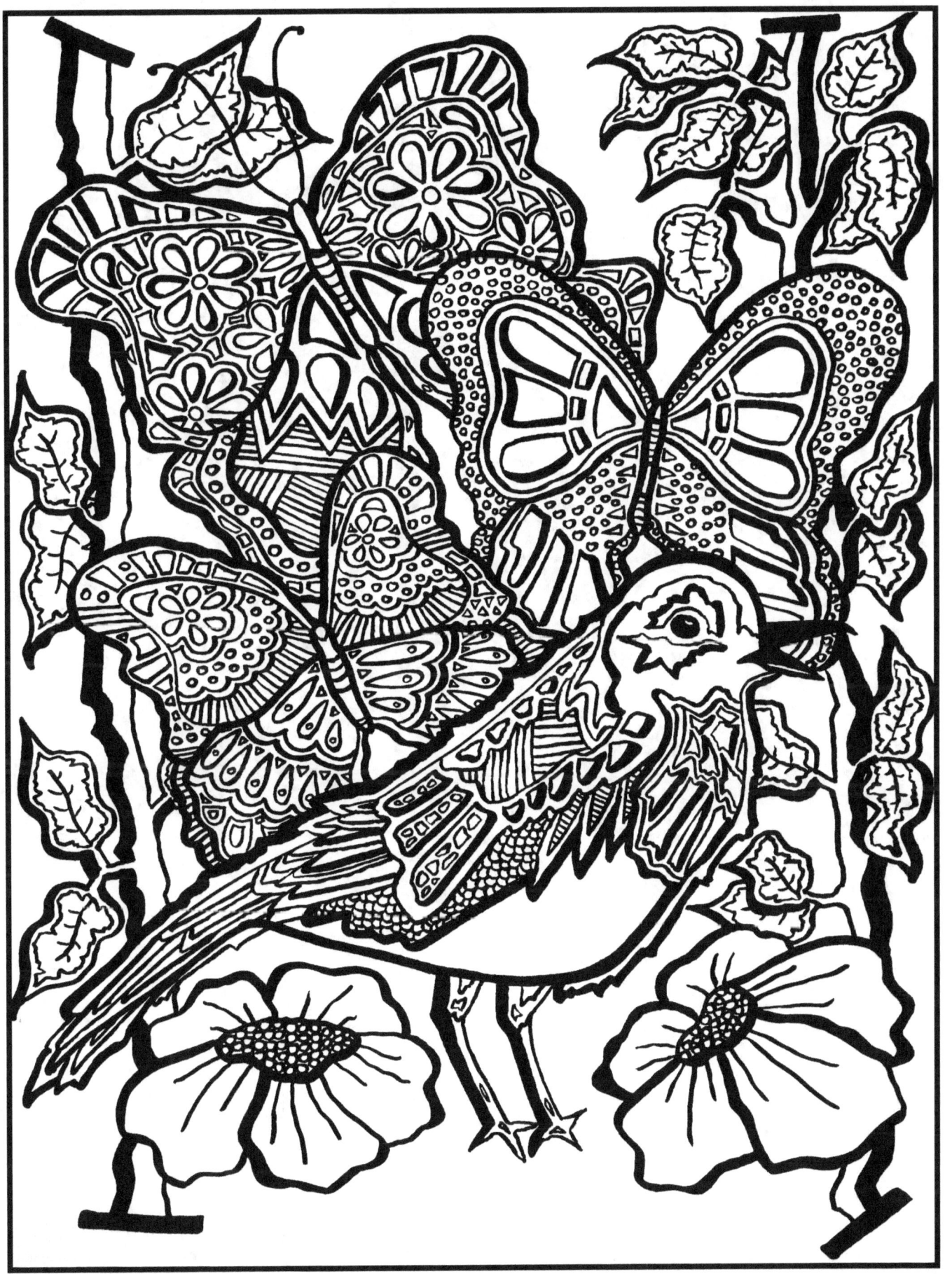

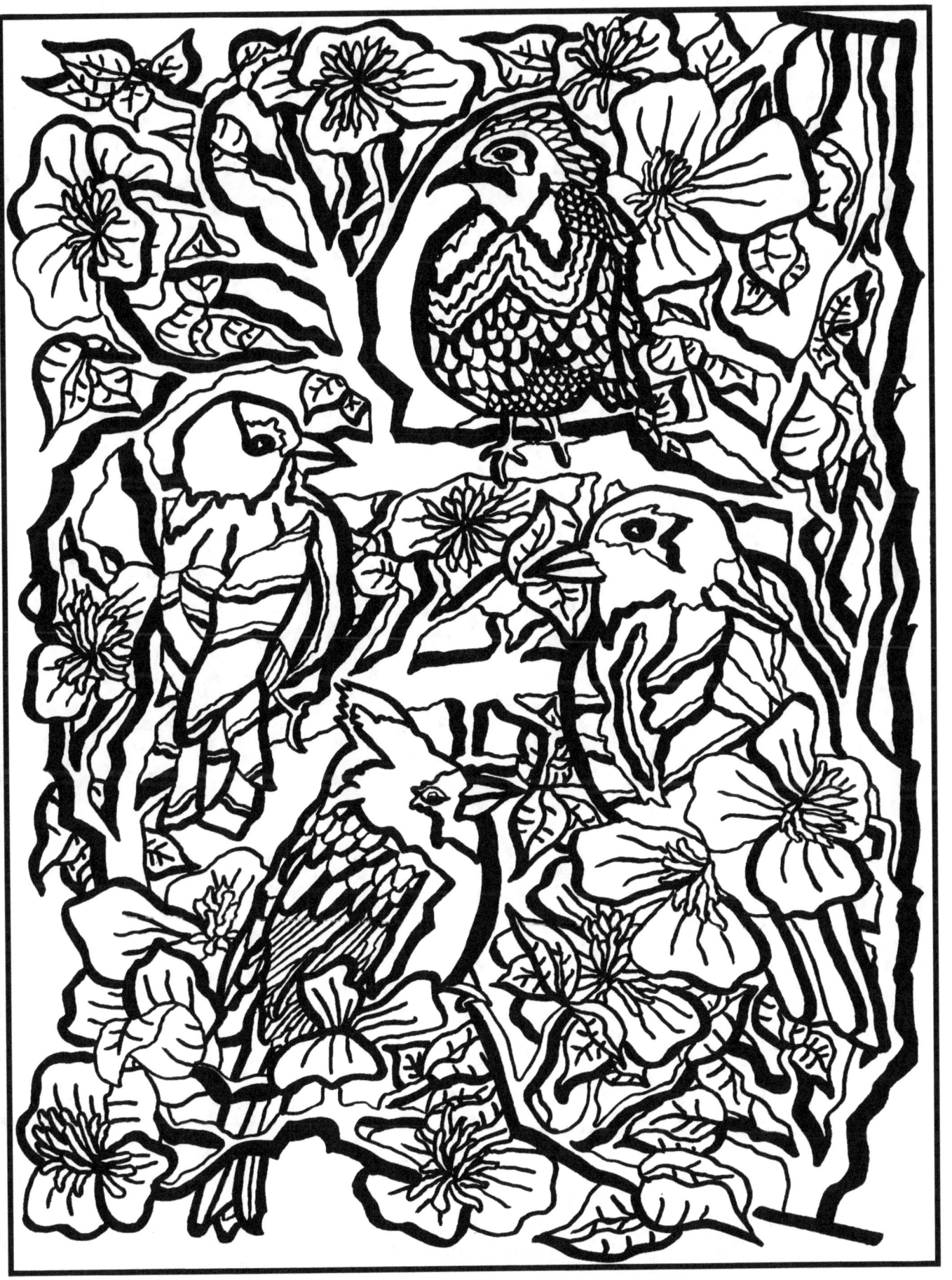

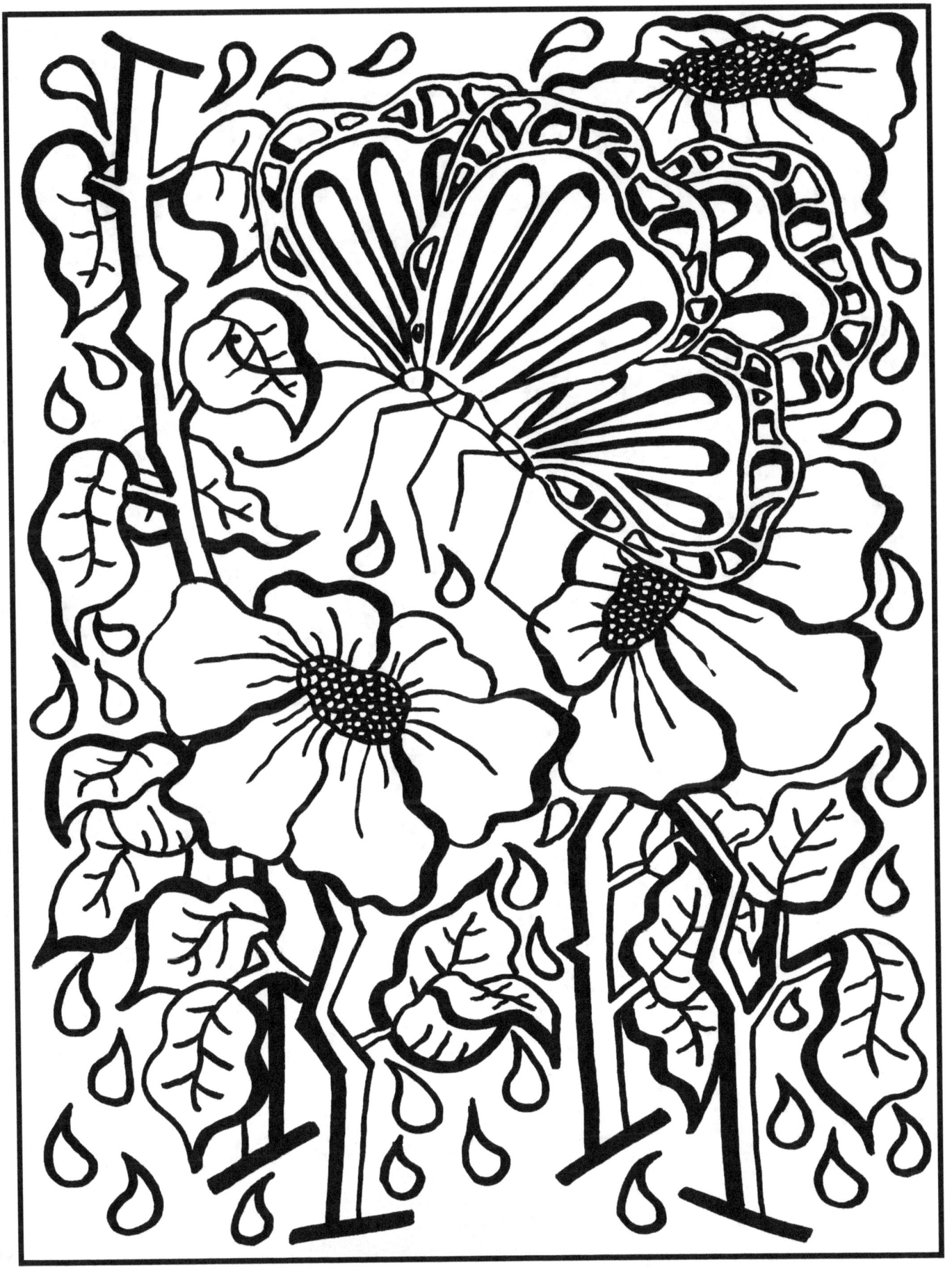

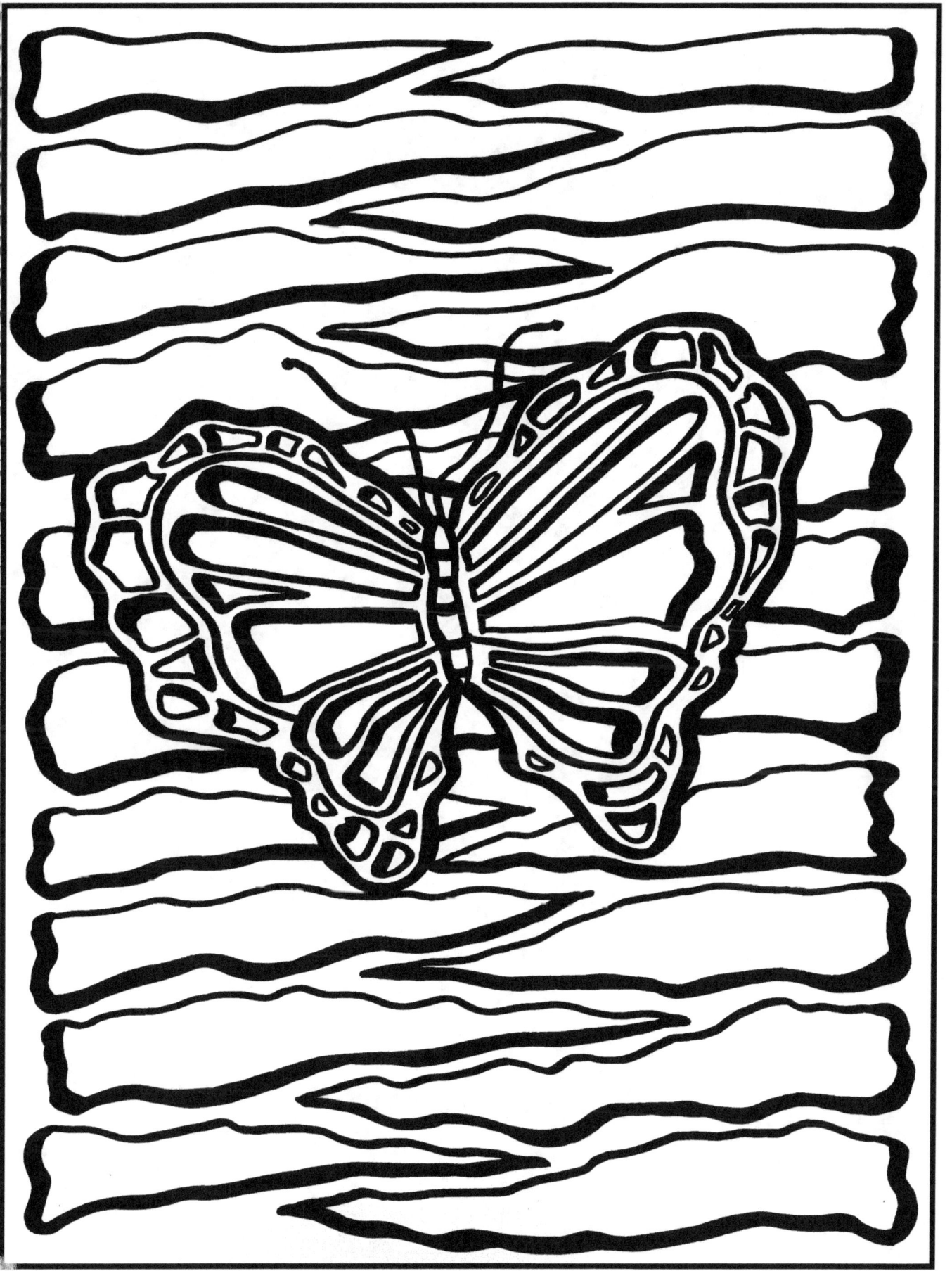

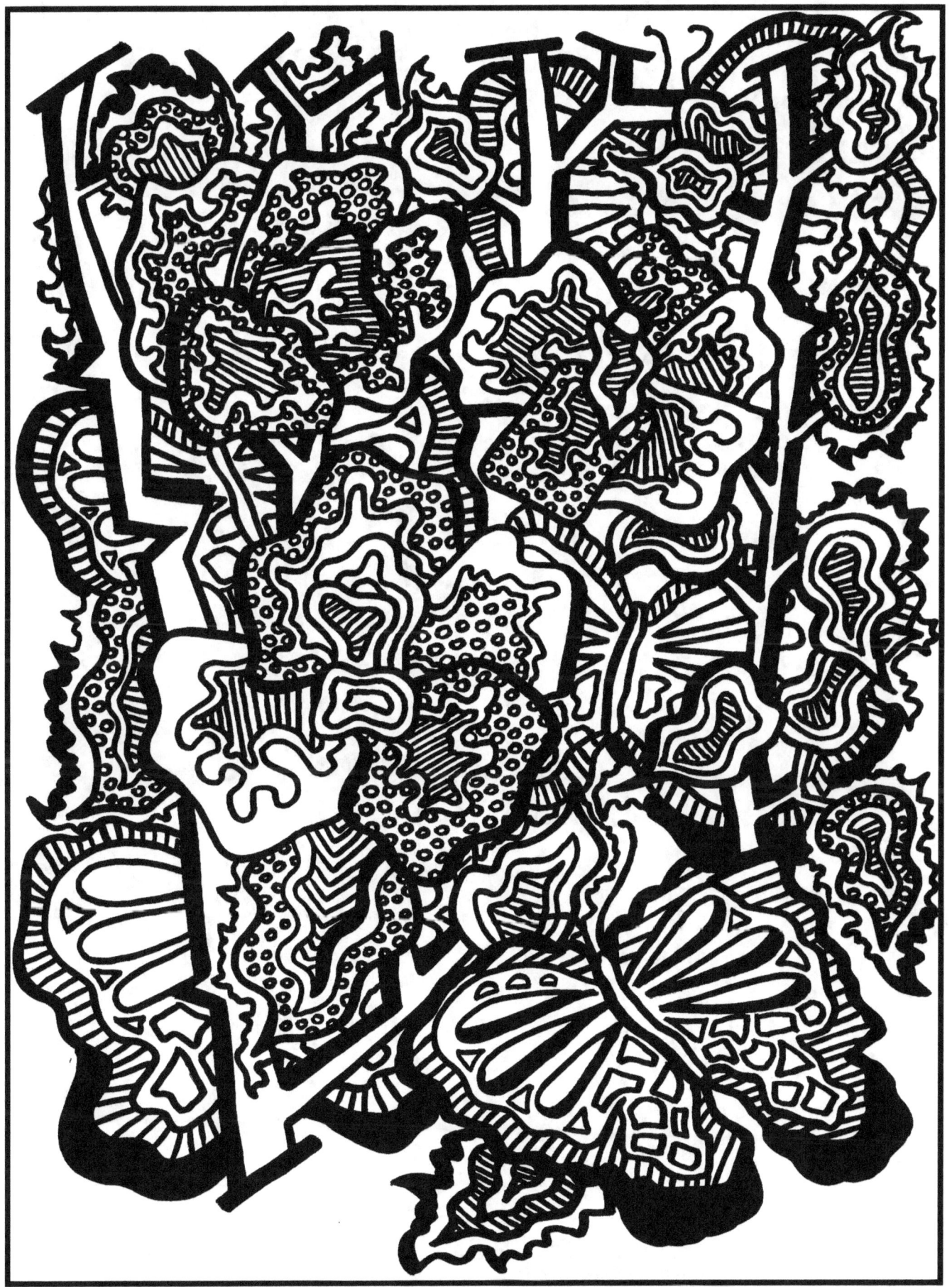

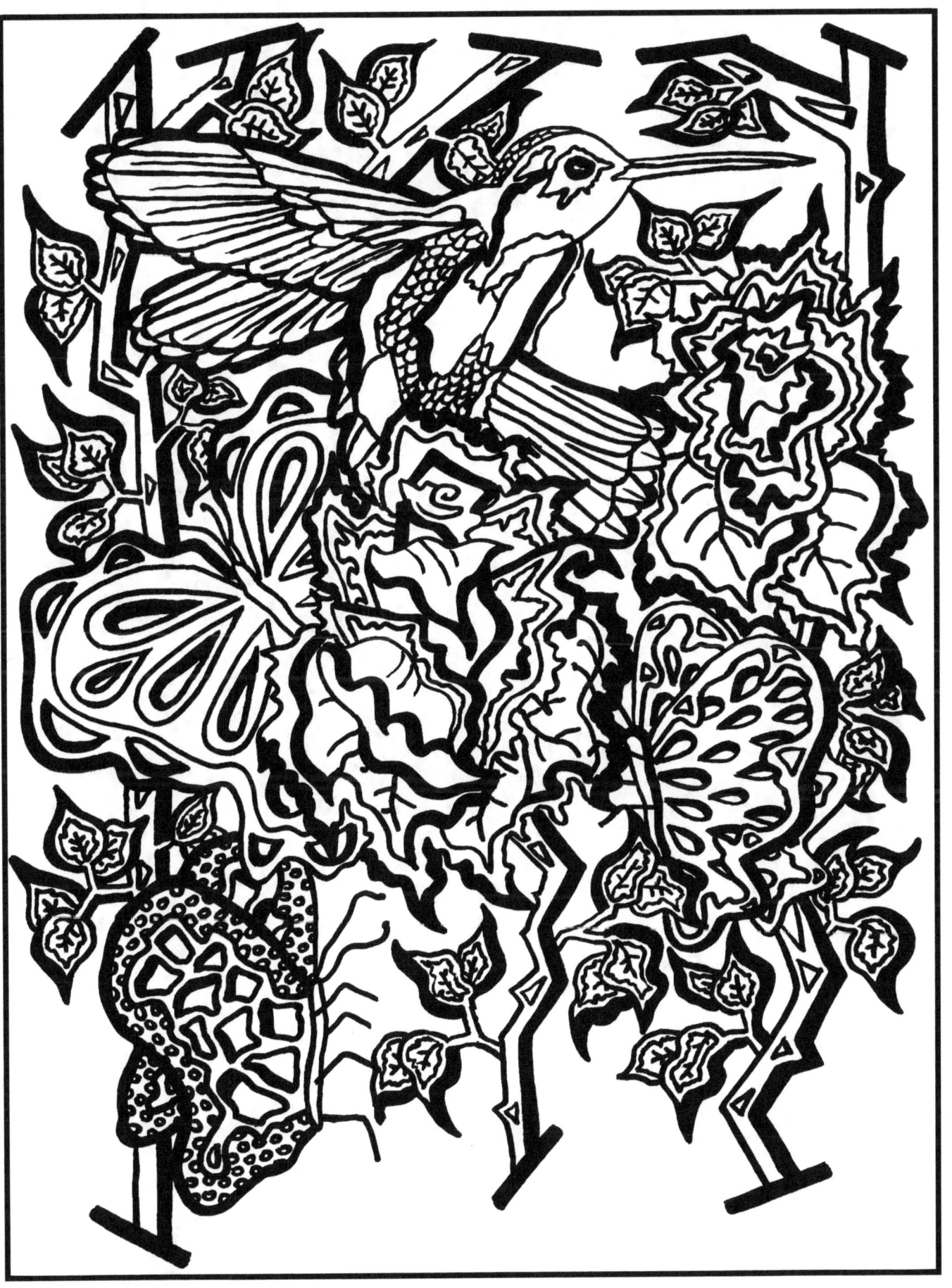

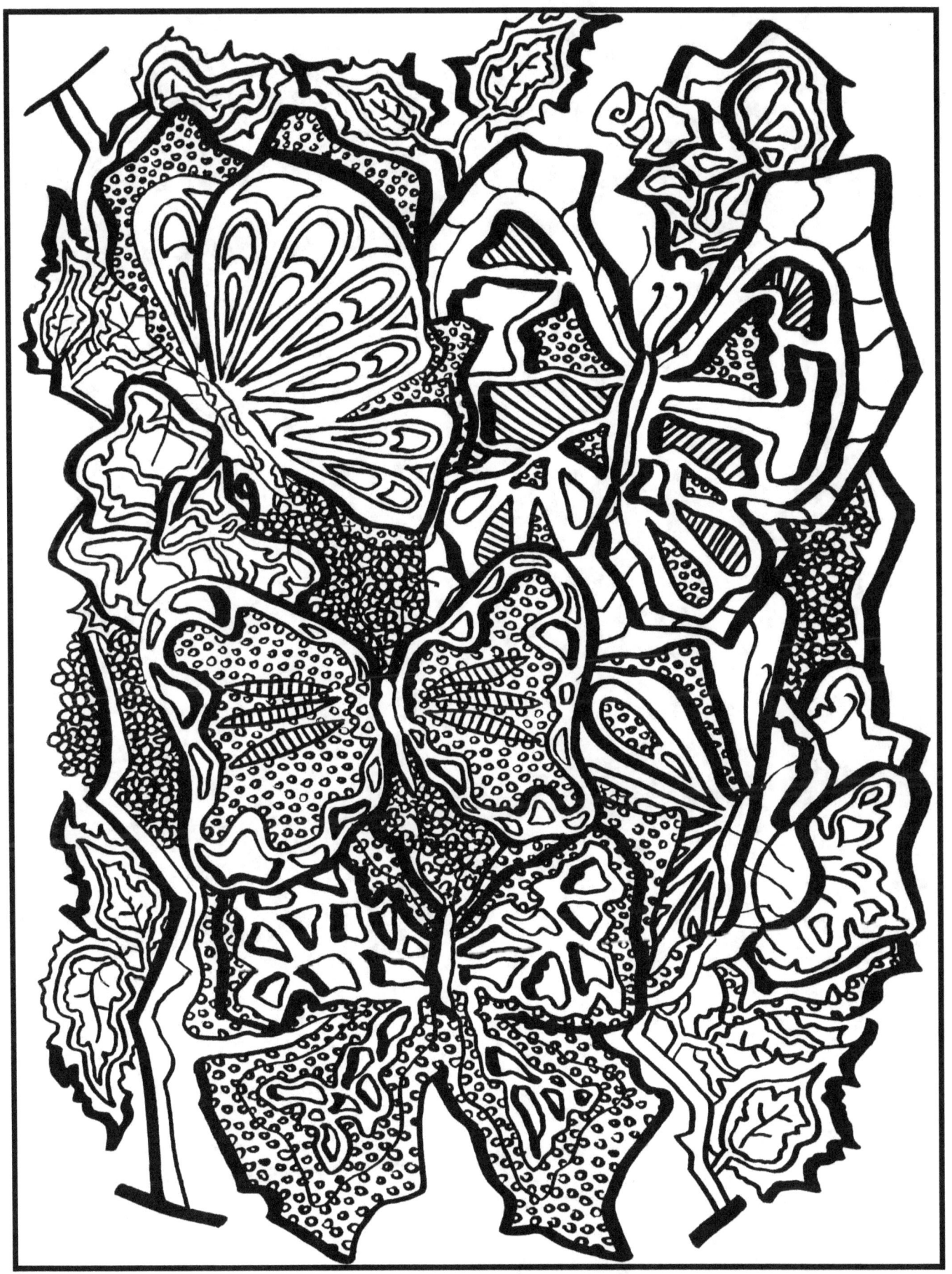

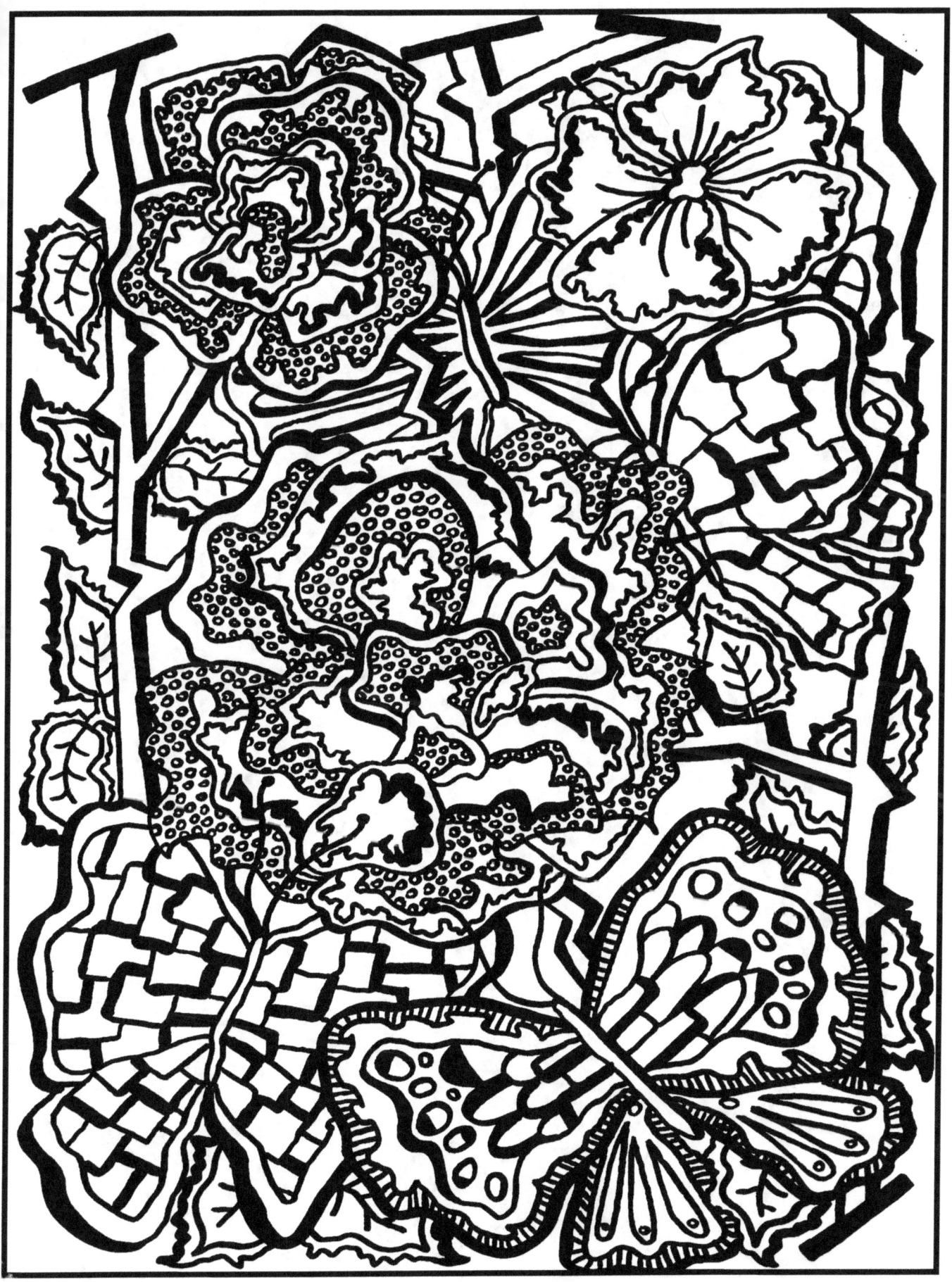

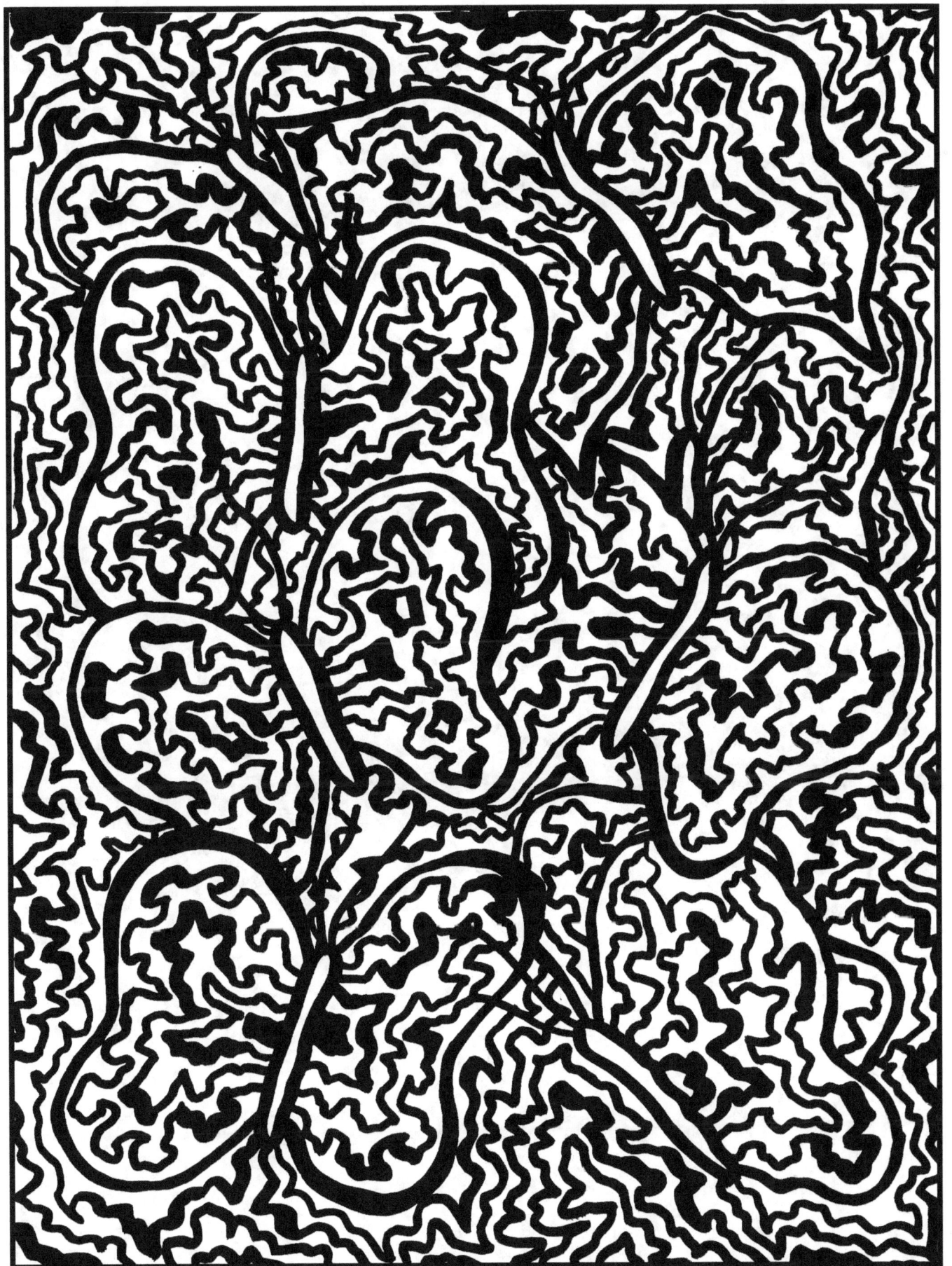

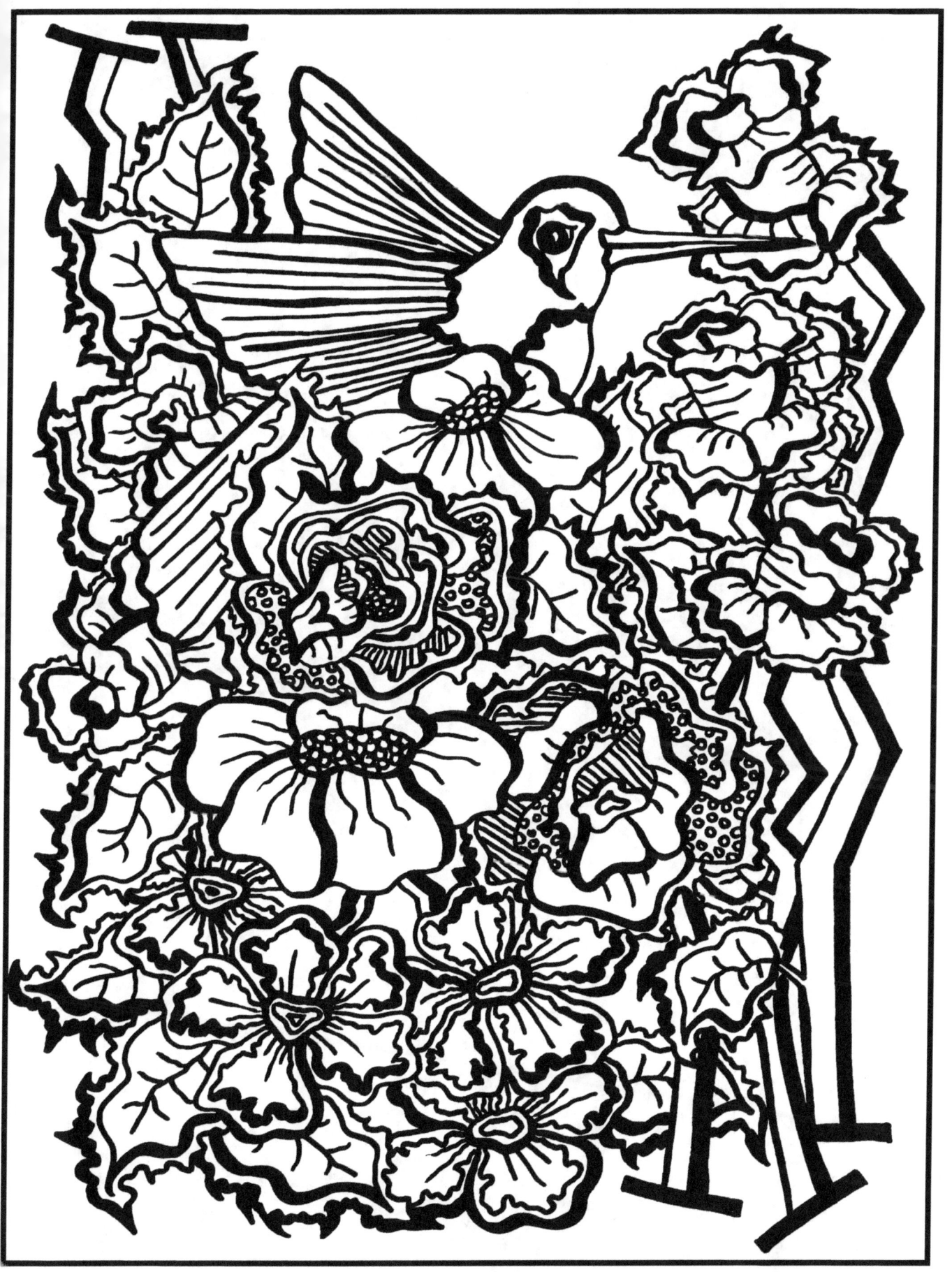

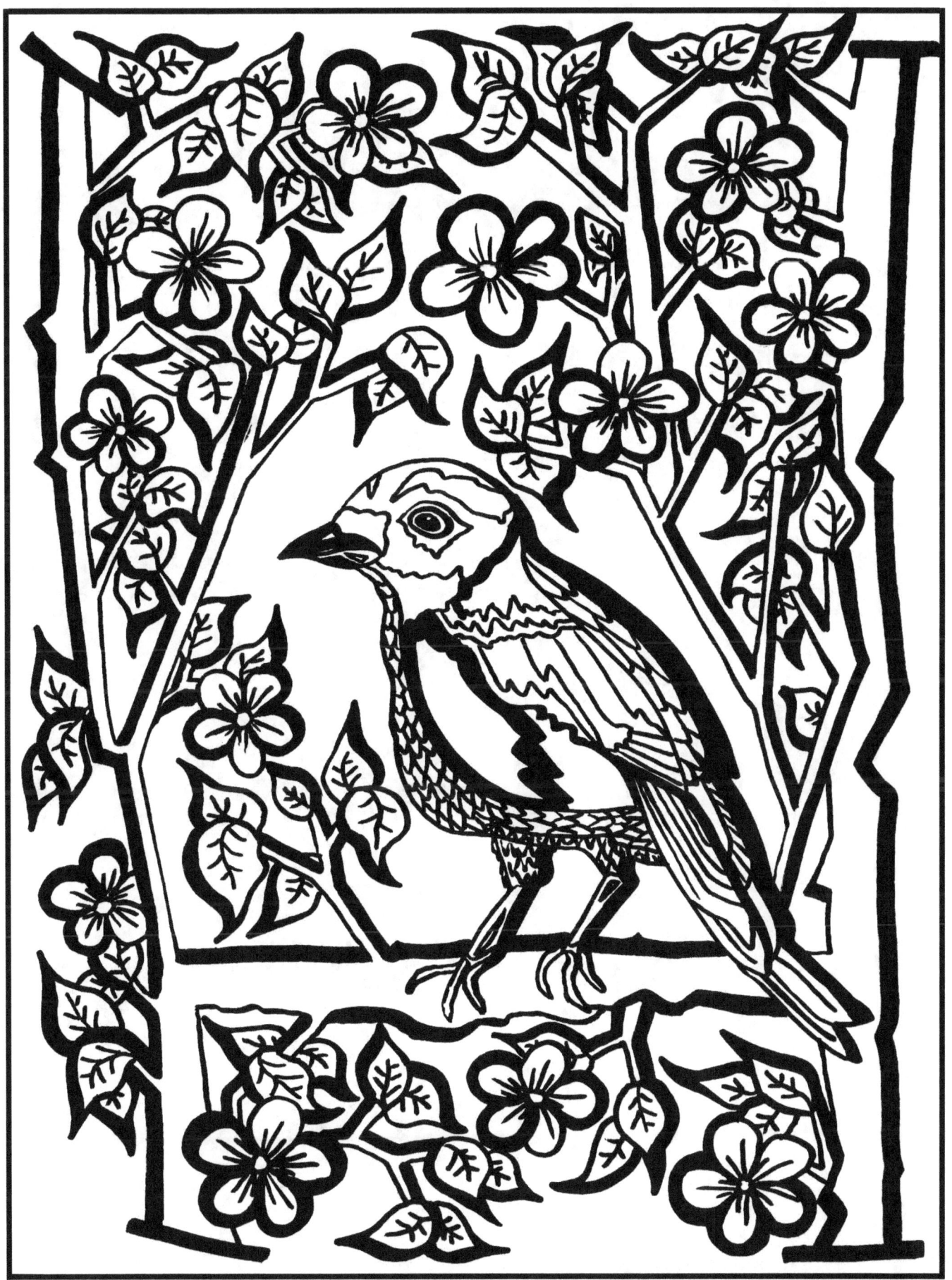

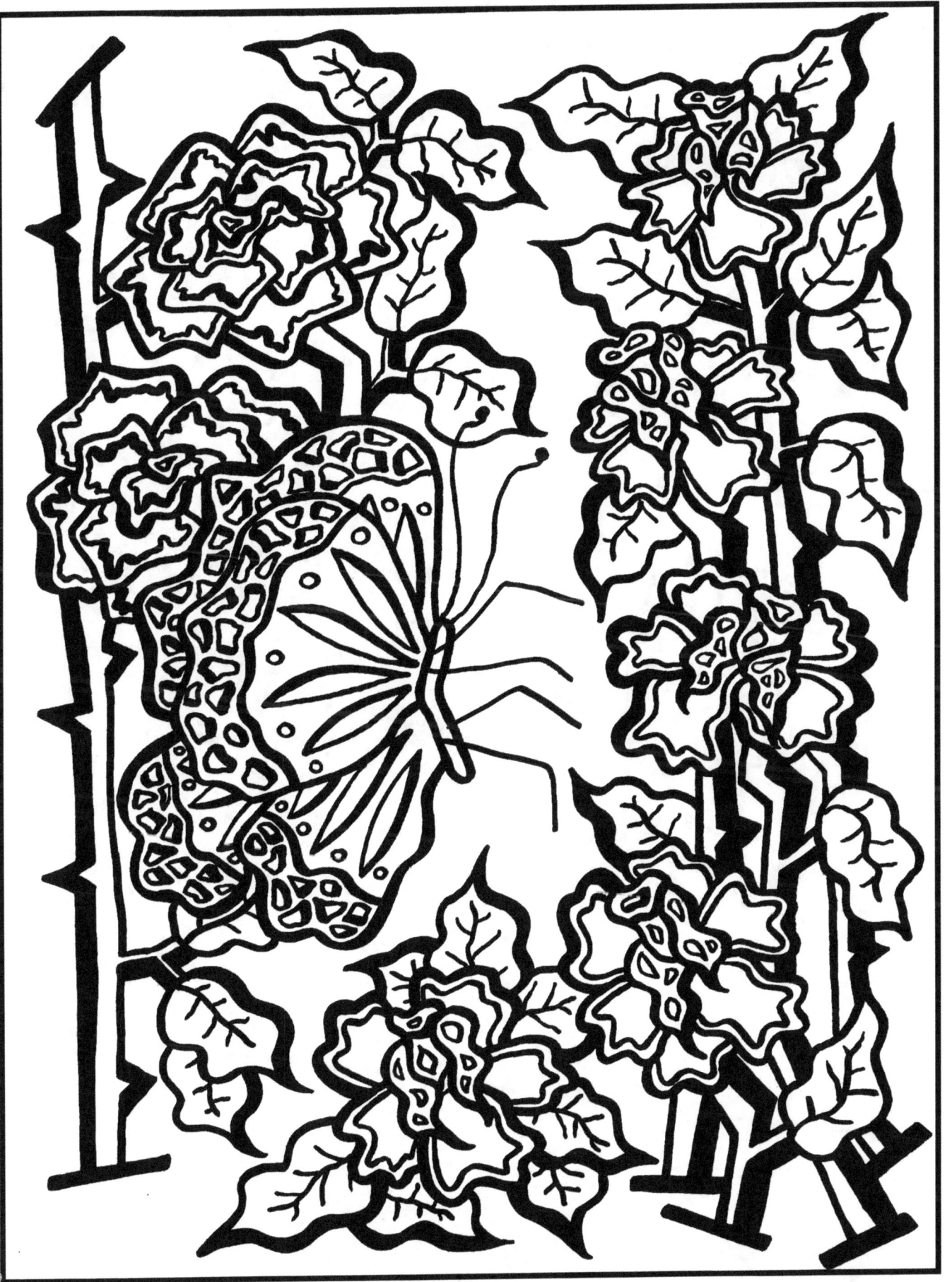

Media Test Page

Media Test Page

Media Test Page

www.ingramcontent.com/pod-product-compliance
Lightning Source LLC
Chambersburg PA
CBHW081608200526
45169CB00021B/2360